Special Signs of Grace

SPECIAL
SIGNS
OF
GRACE

THE SACRAMENTS AND SACRAMENTALS

JOSEPH M. CHAMPLIN

THE LITURGICAL PRESS
Collegeville, Minnesota

Cover design and illustrations by Janice St. Marie

Nihil obstat: Thomas J. Costello, D.D., Auxiliary Bishop of Syracuse, *Censor deputatus.*
Imprimatur: Frank J. Harrison, D.D., Bishop of Syracuse, March 27, 1986.

	2	3	4	5	6	7	8	9

Library of Congress Cataloging in Publication Data
Champlin, Joseph M.
   Special signs of grace.
    1. Sacraments—Catholic Church.   2. Sacramentals.
3. Catholic Church—Doctrines.   I. Title.
BX2200.C385   1986   234´.16   86-10544
ISBN 0-8146-1466-3

In memory of my mother who,
not so much by her words as by her example,
taught me to love the Church and the sacraments.

Contents

Introduction

Ray and Maureen Suatoni could hardly wait for Christmas. While they naturally looked forward to the annual celebration of the Lord's coming as an infant, the young couple, married about four years, felt more anxious about the arrival of their own first child.

The baby, expected December 17, did not appear then. A week later, the pregnant mother and concerned father found their holiday spirits subdued somewhat as they continued to await its birth. Soon afterwards the doctor ordered a Caesarean section and an overdue Ronald Raymond finally entered this world on December 27.

The new parents' joy soon turned into worry when they learned the baby's esophagus and stomach were not connected, a problem necessitating surgery and a complicated recovery process. However, the child's health improved rapidly and within weeks the three of them with relatives, friends, and a favorite priest gathered in the parish church for Ronald's baptism.

On the same afternoon that the Suatonis were celebrating with grateful relief and deep happiness the new life of grace connected with baptism, Bill Regan was making his regular visit to a local health care institution for the elderly. Those trips had become a near daily part of the priest's routine for several years as he watched his mother, nearly eighty-nine, gradually deteriorate, devastated by the ravages of old age.

It was distressful for him to observe this woman suffer sharp pain, occasional disorientation, and frequent frustration. When she died months later in the early fall, he experienced both a peace because that agony had ended and the emptiness of his mother's loss. He had prayed by her side, anointed her with the sacrament of the sick, presented a favorite crucifix for her to kiss, and recited the prayers for the dying into her ear at the very last moments.

Father Regan planned to celebrate the funeral liturgy and, as she had requested, preach the homily. He dreaded doing both and wondered the night before if he would get through them without breaking down. The next morning the relieved, but grieving priest found a spirit of strength and serenity flooded his being as he saw the people assembled in church, heard them sing "The Strife is o'er, the battle won," listened to the Scriptures, and stood at the altar.

Some tears flowed after Communion, but this man found comfort and hope in the prayers' frequent mention of the eternal life now beginning for Dorothy Regan, of a heaven where tears are no more and of an eventual forever reunion with those we love.

The birth of a child and the death of a beloved are obviously major moments in our lives. On those occasions we usually feel quite vulnerable or sensitive to reality and look for a connection between these vital events being experienced and the God whom we worship. We seek insights and strength; we want to express our joy and be consoled in our sorrow.

In between birth and death is a lifetime of other major moments. We grow and graduate; we make mistakes and wish to start over; we fall in love with a person or embrace a way of life; we win victories and suffer defeats; we go through good times and endure bad moments; we enjoy a special occasion and struggle with tedious tasks. In all of these we likewise look for wisdom and courage and try to link the divine Lord with our human lives.

The Catholic Church possesses a rich treasure of resources to help us with this connection and respond to our different needs. Its seven sacraments and many sacramentals provide powerful rituals to aid us in recognizing Christ's presence in the midst of such moments. These rites that appeal to all our senses make an invisible God visibly present in the large and little occasions of our lives.

This book is meant to be a popular, updated explanation of those sacraments and sacramentals. It seeks to weave together on this topic the ancient heritage of Catholic tradition, the current teaching of the Church, and the futuristic thinking of modern theologians.

The first and last chapters are like two book-ends holding together eight small separate, but related volumes. Chapter 1 examines the notions of signs and symbols, concepts essential to an understanding of this subject. Chapter 10, more speculative, abstract, and difficult, is a kind of theological reflection upon what has gone before. Each chapter in between looks at a particular sacrament or the sacramentals. Throughout I have tried to use the rituals themselves as starting points for the discussion, beginning with what we have experienced or what has happened and going on to what lies behind these experiences or happenings.

I am most grateful to Fr. Daniel Durken, O.S.B., and Mr. Mark Twomey of The Liturgical Press who suggested the idea of this book to me and have been very patient with its slow execution as well as helpful with their direction in its development.

Fr. Lawrence Terrien, S.S., professor of theology at St. Patrick's Seminary in Menlo Park, California, made an invaluable suggestion about the arrangement of the material. I wish to express my deep appreciation for that insight.

Four friends read the manuscript and offered excellent criticisms and encouraging support: Francine Bauser, C.S.J., Mrs. Judy Daino, Fr. Donald Krebs, and Fr. John Roark. Their comments were carefully noted in the text's revision and I think greatly improved it. Since there was some disagreement on certain portions, statements, or emphasis, I do not wish to make them accept the responsibility of this book's content, but only to express gratitude for their friendship, for their effort expended in critiquing the text, and for the extremely useful comments sent to me.

Finally, my highly competent personal secretary over the past seven years, Mrs. Patricia Gale, deciphered my increasingly illegible handwriting and speedily converted those-often-hard-to-makeout words into a readable, typed manuscript. I thank her for that and for those years of faithful service.

The Catholic Church's sacraments and sacramentals helped connect a loving God with the Suatonis in their child's difficult birth and with Father Regan in his mother's slow death. I pray that these pages will enable many to make that same connection in the major moments of their lives.

1

More Than Meets the Eye

Colleen McVey and Tony Griffo, a couple in their mid-twenties, stood before the altar of St. John's Church in Liverpool, New York, and promised before priest, relatives, and friends to be true to each other "in good times and in bad, in sickness and in health." With hands joined and facing one another, both then separately added, "I will love you and honor you all the days of my life."

Immediately afterward the best man dug into his pocket, brought forth two gold wedding rings, and placed them on a silver tray for the blessing. After that benediction, Tony took his bride's band, which has "Together for Life" engraved on the inside, slipped it part way upon her third finger, left hand, and said: "Colleen, take this ring as a sign of my love and fidelity. In the name of the Father, and of the Son, and of the Holy Spirit." She drew this gift on the rest of the way symbolizing her acceptance of it and of him, then repeated the procedure with Tony's plain ring.

The Griffos left the next day for a honeymoon in the Caribbean where everyone who spotted those rings immediately understood the simple fact that they were married. However, these bands say more than this to the newlyweds. They symbolize in addition a mysterious bond between them which words cannot describe or define. Moreover, a mere look at or touch of the ring can trigger on the

deepest level within each countless new experiences of love and belonging.

Such ideas and emotions may stem from the past of their relationship, reflect their present experiences or anticipate future events.
Glancing at or fingering the ring can thus stimulate sentiments of
gratitude, generate needed courage, or create hopeful dreams for
tomorrow.

Tony and Colleen tasted the mix of good times and bad almost
from the initial days of their life together and needed the kind of
assistance the wedding ring symbol could provide for them.

Upon return from St. Maertens and the honeymoon, Colleen
remained in Rochester for several months to finish out her contract
with a television station in that city as its news anchorwoman and
producer. Tony, on the other hand, continued to work on Long
Island as an executive in the family cabinet-making business, prepared their future home and traveled extensively around the country for sales purposes. Their moments together during these critical
first months of marriage obviously were irregular, limited, and infrequent. My hunch is that both often touched, looked at, and fin-
gered those gold bands.

Signs, Symbols and Sacraments

Tony and Colleen McVey Griffo get us started with this little book
on the sacraments and sacramentals of the Catholic Church. They
in fact did celebrate, receive, and minister to one another the sacrament of matrimony. They experienced a rich ritual of signs–words,
actions and objects–surrounding the essential exchange of vows between them. They also are aware now and will become even more
conscious later on that this sacramental rite was full of powerful
symbols capable of touching them in a most profound manner.

A subsequent chapter will examine in some detail the sacrament
of matrimony. In the final one we will reflect upon the nature or
essence of a sacrament itself. Here, however, I will comment more
generally about symbols, since all of the sacraments and sacramentals have both a sign and symbolic character to them.

All symbols are signs, but not every sign is a symbol. The meaning of this statement should clarify as we define our use of the words
sign and symbol and describe their meaning through examples.

Signs

A *sign* is a word, an object, or an action which points to something else, leads us to knowledge of something beyond or communicates understanding about a reality hidden from us. Every day our ordinary lives are governed or directed by countless signs.

I get into my car in the morning and printed words tell me to buckle up; the dashboard points out how much gas is in the tank; a blinking red light informs me the vehicle ahead will soon turn right; an arrow warns me this is a one-way street; a green signal moves me ahead; a policeman's outstretched hand motions me to stop; a white cloud rising from the hood spells trouble and leads me to know about an overheated engine; a yellow lamp and barricade communicates to me the reality that the driveway to our parking lot has been torn up; my name over an empty area tells me (and hopefully others) that this is my reserved spot; "exit" shows me the way out at the end of the day.

Many signs are artificial and humanly concocted. As intelligent beings we give an added meaning to words, objects, or actions. "Buckle up," the one-way street arrow, and the policeman's raised arm or hand convey a bit of information, knowledge, or reality beyond what we immediately see, hear, or perceive with our senses. Only humans catch the beyond meaning of such artificial signs. A dog, for example, might be struck and stopped momentarily by the red or green light, but would not understand the further message communicated.

Some signs, however, are natural; they automatically convey the added meaning by their very nature. The smoke or vapor rising from the car hood denotes heat or fire behind it; buds on trees, new green grass all over the ground, and flowers pushing out of the earth tell us spring is here; the smell of steak on a distant charcoal grill gives us a clear picture of the reality we cannot see. A dog, in this case, would probably stay away from the fire or draw nearer to the broiling steak, grasping naturally the meaning of those signs. [1]

Symbols

A *symbol* is a sign. It, therefore, as a word, object, or action points to, leads to, and communicates a reality more than that which our senses immediately perceive. However, it is a special kind of sign with further, deeper meaning. Symbols possess a unique, mysterious power to evoke conscious and unconscious thoughts and feelings within us. Those ideas and emotions have a connection with and are triggered by the symbols, but go much beyond them.

Tony and Colleen exchanged wedding rings. All could and can see the gold bands on the couple's fingers. Our society has, however, in addition given a sign value to these rings: they indicate that those wearing them are married. But such nuptial bands are, moreover, symbols as well, rich and powerful in their ability to stir the inner self.

On certain occasions, for example, the ring may bring back memories of a day early in their courtship when they spent hours walking the streets of New York just talking, talking, talking as new lovers do; it may make very real to one of them at a particular moment the greatness of the other's love; it may beget at another time peace and reassurance as it speaks of the other's commitment for life regardless of the daily ups and downs surrounding their marital existence.

This illustration of the Griffos underscores a special element in all symbols. They possess a past, present, and future dimension to them.

Some Characteristics of Symbols

But there are many other fascinating characteristics about symbols. As we sketch a few of these ingredients and amplify the explanation with examples, the nature of symbols should appear in sharper focus. Nevertheless, we must in a sense stand back in awe of symbols, since they are mysterious and cannot be fully grasped. [2]

Signs generally give information; symbols beget inspiration.

An "exit" sign points the way out of a theater; it communicates information, but does not stir our inner feelings or trigger the imagination. On the other hand, should a fire develop during the performance and we must crawl out of the smoke-filled auditorium, sighting the exit sign would give us hope and renewed determination. The sign has now become a symbol of air, freedom, escape, and safety; as a symbol it has stirred our inner selves and provided not simply information, but inspiration.

Symbols disclose part of another reality without communicating the total dimension of it.

Such a partial disclosure both helps and hurts us, is a cause of both joy and sorrow, both satisfies and frustrates us. Tony and Colleen will hold hands, kiss, and make love to one another. These will express in an external, physical way their deeper, inner feelings. Becoming two in one flesh will help their relationship, bring them great joy, and satisfy one another. But at the same time, this love making will never fully capture what one wishes to say to the other, whether it be "I love you" or "I am sorry" or "I am scared" or "I am pleased and grateful" or "I understand." That inability hurts, makes us sad as we realize our human limitations and brings on frustration.

Symbols make the other reality present without being identical to it.

No doubt Colleen and Tony carry photographs of each other in their wallets, images of the other, an accurate likeness of the spouse in some particular setting. Shown to an interested viewer, the snapshot gives a good representation and is a fine sign. But during the extended separation in the early days of their marriage, the same photo was probably looked at with love and perhaps even kissed. It then became a symbol, in its own way making the other present, despite the fact it obviously is not the actual spouse. [3]

Symbols can reveal or conceal, serve as a bridge or a screen.

People who have the ability to look beyond the sign or symbol gain entrance to an added reality; for those who do not have that ability, the sign or symbol stops them at the external level. For example, friends or relatives may admire the photographic image of Tony or Colleen, but it does not move those people as much as the identical picture with its symbolic power touches the young spouses. So, too, in the religious realm, faith is that ability to penetrate further. People with faith look beyond bread, wine, and water in the Eucharist to reach another reality, Christ concealed behind the elements; those lacking faith see only bread, wine, and water. [4]

Symbols bring us into touch with realities in our lives which are at one and the same time familiar and mysterious.

The lives of Tony and Colleen Griffo converged to form a love story. We are all familiar with such love tales and have been involved with many loves in our own lives. But the love experience and the nature of love remain mysterious. We cannot explain love, analyze it, reason it away. Through symbols this elusive and mysterious love becomes more familiar to us; we can better grasp it; we are able in some degree to get this into our heads and hearts.

Symbols seem to be born, then grow, and sometimes die when the situation changes.

Marriage Encounter flourished about a decade ago. Almost every weekend couples in great numbers went away to a hotel, motel, or retreat house and there most experienced a sort of rebirth of their marital love. It was common to see in those days spouses coming to the altar for Communion holding hands, mixing with other encountered couples afterwards, and bearing the Marriage Encounter heart and cross symbol on their car's rear window. When Marriage Encounter couples passed an auto with a similar sticker, they would honk, wave, and smile. Its presence triggered a host of positive inner sentiments.

The movement has now crested and, while still alive, one sees fewer and fewer Encounter stickers on cars. Moreover, sight of the symbol probably does not engender the same intense interior reactions among Marriage Encounter veterans that it did several years ago. Symbols are born, flourish, and sometimes die when the situation changes.[5]

Symbols have many layers of meaning and take time to develop.

Thanksgiving and Christmas are in fact symbolic days for Americans. An outside observer might seek to discover the essential element of these celebrations and conclude that it was the turkey for one and Santa Claus for the other. But we know that both holidays have much more to them than the stuffed bird or a bearded bearer of gifts.

Preparations for Christmas, fortunately or unfortunately, begin a few weeks prior to Thanksgiving when decorations appear on city shopping streets; they continue with busy shopping sprees on the Friday and Saturday after Thanksgiving; radios play "I'll be home for Christmas" over and over again throughout December setting off happy anticipatory thoughts in people at home or far away; writing cards and receiving them, wrapping presents and delivering them, hosting parties and attending them are all part of the picture; perhaps "going to confession," or Midnight Mass, or just having the family together at church on Christmas become traditions for some; an atmosphere of stockings, trees, lights, and carols surround us; picking up family members at airports, train stations, or bus depots, opening presents, eating the big dinner, visiting both sets of parents and collapsing in happy, relieved fatigue at the day's end are commonplace events near and on the holiday itself.

Beyond those externals are feelings and thoughts, too numerous, fleeting, and complex to even list, but usually of a bittersweet mixture which accompany our preparation and celebration of Christmas. The same holds true, but to a lesser extent for Thanksgiving. The symbolic richness of these days is many-layered, but the complexity and depth of those symbols have taken years to evolve. For our society and for the individual person, each year's celebration adds to that richness.[6]

Symbols possess a hidden, mysterious power to evoke conscious and unconscious responses within us.

Jesuit theologian Avery Dulles in his classic book *Models of the Church* discusses in a perceptive, even if technical way, this evocative power of symbols. Noting that the psychology of images is exceedingly subtle and complex, he describes how in the religious sphere images function as symbols. They consequently speak to us existentially and find an echo in the inarticulate depths of our psyches. Such images communicate through their evocative power. They convey a latent meaning that is apprehended in a nonconceptual, even a subliminal way. Symbols transform the horizons of our lives, integrate our perception of reality, alter our scale of values, reorient our loyalties, attachments, and aspirations in a manner far exceeding the powers of abstract conceptual thought.

According to Dulles, religious images, as used in the Bible and Christian preaching, focus our experience in a new way. They have an aesthetic appeal, and are apprehended not simply by the mind but by the imagination, the heart, or, more properly, the whole person:

> Any large and continuing society that depends on the loyalty and commitment of its members requires symbolism to hold it together. In secular life, we are familiar with the bald eagle, the black panther, the fleur-de-lis. These images respectively arouse courage, militancy, and purity. The biblical images of the Church as the flock of Christ, the Bride, the Temple, or whatever, operate in a similar manner. They suggest attitudes and courses of action; they intensify confidence and devotion. To some extent they are self-fulfilling; they make the Church become what they suggest the Church is.[7]

Two Illustrations

The following different, but related incidents may serve to exemplify in a connected way the multiple and diverse dimensions of symbols.

One evening in between dinner and an early appointment I flipped on television to catch a bit of the news. Watching this report is not a part of my regular routine, and consequently I had not settled in for an accustomed half hour or so of viewing. On the contrary I was sitting on the edge of a chair for some reason wishing to catch a minute or so of the telecast before resuming work.

It was then a day or two after that Beirut bombing in which several hundred Marines had lost their lives during a suicide terrorist action. The program this night showed clips from a hangar at the Dover Air Force Base in Delaware, film footage covering the military honors which surrounded the return of a few recovered bodies from Lebanon.

I suddenly became glued to the set. The flag-draped coffins, the honor guard's precision marching, the funeral music by the military band, the full dress soldiers at attention, the brief, consoling message from a commanding officer, the survivors' pained faces and courageous words—all these elements swiftly engaged my interest and drew me deeply into the event. Feelings of grief and sadness started in my stomach and rose to my head; my eyes watered; confused thoughts raced in my mind. The coverage lasted for five minutes at the maximum, but those sights and sounds, the words, the objects and the actions of that ritual ceremony touched me profoundly.

Why? I knew none of the deceased Marines nor any of the survivors. But somehow that service, symbolic in itself and filled with different, potent symbols, triggered reactions within me. Did it recall the tear-filled hours I spent years ago watching on television the funeral of our assassinated President John F. Kennedy? Was it the grief of the present, the tragedy of the moment, the courage of the soldiers or the plight of the relatives before me? Could it have reminded me of my own mortality and future death?

Around the same time at a main Marine base in the South, a similar drama took place. A widow of one victim stood with a preschool son beside the coffin of her husband and his father. Following the burial prayers, a presiding general (actually the fallen Marine's father) presented with the customary message first a folded flag to the widow and then a smaller one to the son. The youngster, confused by all the happenings up to this point, took the triangular red, white, and blue bundle, held it for a moment, and finally pressed it to his heart. That symbol seemed to say it all for him, somehow summed up the unfathomable mysteries of love, life, and death he was experiencing and brought those familiar, but elusive realities into clearer perspective for his mind and heart.

A Foundation for What Follows

I hope this lengthy treatment of signs and symbols establishes a firm foundation for the chapters which follow.

A person cannot understand the Catholic Church otherwise because its life and worship are filled with countless such visible pointers or reflectors leading us to a knowledge of realities beyond what our senses apprehend. In fact Baptist theologian Langdon Gilkey, while probing to discover the distinctive identity of Catholicism, listed the symbolic or sacramental emphasis in the Church as one of its essential characteristics. He sees in the Catholic Church a "continuing experience, unequalled in other forms of Western Christianity, of the presence of God and of grace mediated through symbols to the entire course of ordinary human life."[8]

Furthermore, the seven Catholic sacraments are actually unique signs or symbols of grace handed down to us by Christ through his Church. As we will see in our treatment of each one, they are special signs—words, objects and actions—which point to something else, lead us to a knowledge beyond and communicate an understanding of a further reality.

Moreover, the sacraments and sacramentals are, in addition, symbols. Therefore, they:

—possess a past, present, and a future
—beget inspiration, disclose part of another reality without conveying the total dimension of it
—make the other reality present without being identical to it
—can reveal or conceal
—bring us in touch with realities in our lives which are simultaneously familiar and mysterious
—have many layers of meaning
—took time to develop
—can change in certain aspects of their celebration
—and possess a hidden, mysterious power to evoke conscious and unconscious responses within us.

Necessary Dispositions

For those signs/symbols/sacraments to exert their fullest impact, nevertheless, we need a sense of awe, ample time to savor the symbolic experience and, above all, a faith which penetrates beyond the sign to the deeper reality.

A sense of *awe* lifts us out of the modern materialistic, consumer-oriented, measurable mentality, which judges only as reality objects which can be perceived with our senses, purchased for use, or measured by computerized instruments. The human individual, whether as unborn child in the womb, paralyzed octogenarian at a nursing home, or disagreeable neighbor down the street, may be viewed as merely such an object (even disposable) or seen with awe as a body and spirit person of infinite worth.

We need ample time to savor a symbolic event for its full impact. When 750 people bring forward to the altar at a Thanksgiving Day Mass bags and cartons of food for the poor, the procession can be a mechanical, confused, rushed, get-it-over-with action or a reverent, orderly, unhurried, and loving experience. The $1,000 of groceries mounted in the sanctuary will aid the same number of hungry, hurting people, but the participants who carried up the gifts will be touched more deeply by the leisurely paced procession of food parcels to the altar than by the rapidly discharged deposit of the thousand items in the sanctuary.

Most critically, however, faith *is that which enables a person to look beyond the signs or symbols and discover something more.* Our senses stop at bread, wine, water, oil, hands, words or actions. Our faith goes further and reaches the deeper, concealed reality.

For many years, the Dameans, a group of musically talented priests originally from a New Orleans seminary, composed, recorded, and played songs that have become standard fare for Catholic liturgies and prayer services. One of their earlier compositions, published in 1969, is called "Look Beyond"; its refrain brings this chapter to a close:

> Look beyond the bread you eat
> See your Savior and your Lord.
> Look beyond the Cup you drink
> See his love poured out as blood.[9]

We will now look beyond seven special signs or symbols of grace and seek to discover the reality present to us through those Catholic sacraments.

Discussion Questions

1. How would you describe or define a "sign"?
2. Make a list of ten signs which are a part of your everyday life and indicate which are natural and which are humanly concocted, for example, smoke and "exit."
3. How would you describe or define a "symbol"?
4. Identify a symbol personal to you which, like a wedding ring or a photograph, has a past, present, and future dimension to it.
5. Recall an incident in your life when you used some type of symbol, like a letter or a gift, which disclosed part of your thoughts or feelings to another or others, but could not fully and satisfactorily communicate all of your thoughts or the total depth of your feelings.

6. Can you think of a symbol which has real meaning for you, but means nothing to someone else? In other words, it is a bridge and reveals for you, but conceals and is a screen for others.
7. Reflect a bit on either Thanksgiving or Christmas and note how many elements you connect with its celebration or how many layers of meaning the feast or holiday has for you and how long it has taken to develop those multiple levels of meaning.
8. Are you able to remember an occasion when some symbol, like a trumpet playing at a funeral or the reunion of two separated lovers in a movie, triggered a reaction inside of you and even brought tears to your eyes?
9. Describe a situation in which you experienced a sense of awe and wonder, like the birth of a baby or a particularly beautiful sunset.
10. When you receive Communion or penance, what does your faith tell you is happening?

BAPTISM:

a
new life
and
a new
family

2

Baptism: A New Life and a New Family

While many might judge Christmas to be the most significant day of the Roman Catholic liturgical year, in point of fact Easter is the central celebration around which all others revolve. The original, oldest and for a time the only feast, Easter recalls in living fashion Jesus' Paschal or Passover mystery of his coming, dying, rising, and coming again. In similar fashion, while Midnight Mass on December 25 may attract crowds and appear as the year's spiritual highpoint, the vigil celebration on Holy Saturday evening or early Easter morning holds a loftier position in the Church's life.

It is then we celebrate the Lord's resurrection. It is then we end the annual Lenten retreat by renewing our baptismal promises to cast aside sin's darkness and cling to Christ's light. It is then through profession of faith, baptism, confirmation, and first reception of the Eucharist that new adult members are initiated into the Church, welcomed to the Christian community and become part of our spiritual family.

All of this is a relatively new practice, although with deep roots in our ancient past. The Church prior to and after the Second Vatican Council revised the Holy Saturday liturgy both in content and location. In addition, it developed the new Rite of Christian Initiation of Adults (RCIA) which culminates with the reception of adults into the Church during the Easter Vigil.

The RCIA

The Rite of Christian Initiation of Adults requires that adults who seek to enter the Catholic Church normally must pass through a series of stages designed to inform them about the teachings of the Church and form them according to the principles of Christian living. Those periods or stages include:

The precatechumenate: A time in which the person first hears the gospel, undergoes an initial conversion, makes some inquiries about the Church, and decides to look more seriously into this matter by entering the order of catechumens. That period, as should be evident, has no specific time parameters, but varies according to the inspirations of God through grace.

The catechumenate: A segment, on some occasions lasting for several years, but more often extending from the fall until Ash Wednesday, when a person is enrolled as a catechumen, undergoes more formal instruction, grows in faith, experiences several special liturgical rites and finally, at the beginning of Lent, is "elected" as a suitable candidate for membership in the Church.

The purification, enlightenment, or illumination period: A time, generally of a few weeks' duration and usually within Lent, when the candidate by instruction and special rituals (called "scrutinies") undergoes a deeper spiritual preparation for entrance into the Church.

The initiation itself: Normally at the Easter vigil, an event when the elect through the initiation sacraments of baptism, confirmation, and the Eucharist come forward and, "with their sins forgiven, are admitted into the people of God, receive the adoption of the sons of God, and are led by the Holy Spirit into the promised fullness of time and, in the eucharistic sacrifice and meal, to the banquet of the Kingdom of God."[1]

The postbaptismal or "mystagogical" period: a segment, ordinarily extending throughout the Easter season, when new members of the Church deepen their Christian experience, gain spiritual fruit and enter more closely into the life and unity of the community of the faithful.[2]

The RCIA provides for adults who wish to become Roman Catholics, but the Church also baptizes infants and likewise has a ritual for them revised after the Second Vatican Council. However, this rite, too, links together Easter, the death/resurrection of Christ and baptism. To illustrate such a connection, the Church recommends that baptisms whenever possible be celebrated at the

Easter vigil or on Sundays, since every Sunday is a "little Easter" at which we recall the Lord's resurrection.[3]

While in the first years of Christianity those being initiated were mostly adults, the Church has from its earliest times baptized children as well as adults.[4] The rest of this chapter centers on the ritual and regulations of infant baptism as the focal point for our discussion about the outward sign, institution of, and effects of that sacrament.

Since baptism forms a part of the RCIA, as we have seen above, the detailed comments which follow about various elements of the baptismal liturgy apply, although with adaptations, to the celebration of baptism within the context of the RCIA process.

The essential part of baptism is quite simple: the baptizing person (ordinarily a bishop, priest, or deacon) either pours water over the candidate's head or immerses the individual for the fuller meaning of the sign of dying and rising in a baptismal pool pronouncing the words: "I baptize you in the name of the Father, and of the Son, and of the Holy Spirit."[5] However, the reasons behind these fundamental elements and the rites which have come to surround them are numerous, rich, and complex.

Water

Water does many things and, as a result, becomes a sign or symbol of various realities beyond itself. Water cleanses, refreshes and gives life, among other effects, but also can destroy and bring death. It should not be surprising, therefore, that ancient religions employed water in their rituals as a sign of spiritual cleansing, of energy regeneration, and of initiation into a new life or leaving aside an old way of living.

In the Hebew Scriptures or Old Testament, we read often about prescribed water washings; we also know that a Jewish sect around the time of Christ called the Essenes regularly performed a cleansing ritual with water; finally, the Gospels speak of John the Baptist's baptism of repentance, a water rite signifying a person's change of heart and willingness to live a new life.

While there is an uncertainty about whether Jesus ever baptized or not, his institution of the sacrament and the words attributed to him in the Scriptures about baptism would as a consequence have been familiar terms and easily understood by people of that day. Christ's message then and now deals with cleansing, new life, and death to old ways.[6]

Moreover, the Church sees in its use of water for baptism an element which recalls great happenings in the past, occasions when God used water in powerful fashion with humankind. They include the creation of the world (Gen 1-2); Noah and the Ark (Gen 6-9); the Passover deliverance through the Red Sea (Exod 14-15); the desert rock giving forth water (Exod 17; Num 20); the crossing of the Jordan into the promised land (Josh 3); the promises of different prophets that God will pour out water upon the chosen people, a symbol of the Holy Spirit's outpouring (Ezek 36; Isa 35, 44); John's baptism which Jesus received at the start of his ministry (Matt 3). Both the Easter vigil and the baptismal liturgies refer frequently to these and other similar texts.

The word "baptize" itself comes from a Greek root which means to dip in or under or to immerse rather than to cleanse or wash. The Church actually today prefers immersion to infusion, the dipping or submerging of infant or adult into water rather than a mere pouring, because the former is a more suitable sign of participating in the death and resurrection of Christ. A growing number of parish churches have constructed larger baptismal fonts with flowing water especially designed for that purpose. [7]

Trinity

Throughout the Acts of the Apostles, we discover repeated, similar references to baptism in the early Church. [8] In the first instance, Peter proposes a course of action to the crowd deeply shaken by Pentecost's events and his explanation of those happenings. When these people ask him what they should do, he responds: "You must reform and be baptized, each one of you, in the name of Jesus Christ, that your sins may be forgiven; then you will receive the gift of the Holy Spirit (2:38)."

The phrase "to be baptized in the name of Jesus," which occurs in all those cases of baptism within Acts, has a particular meaning. It above all distinguishes the Christian baptismal ritual from other similar washing rites in existence at the time. However, the expression "in the name of" also denotes in both the original Greek and Aramaic languages ownership or a status of personal relationship often connected with slavery.

Thus to be baptized in the name of Jesus signifies entering into Christ's service, developing a personal relationship with him as Lord and Master, becoming his follower, taking his name, being known as a Christian, and formally bringing about or establishing this connection with Jesus. [9]

After his resurrection, Christ commissioned the eleven apostles to go forth and make disciples of all nations. In this process they were to

"Baptize them in the name 'of the Father, and of the Son, and of the Holy Spirit' " (Matt 28:19).

The baptismal ritual we employ today reflects those words of the Lord and includes that Trinitarian formula. It signifies, consequently, that the newly baptized are expressing their faith in the Trinity as well, entering into a relationship of love with the Three Persons, becoming a member of that divine family, and committing themselves to the glory and power of the Most Holy Trinity.[10]

Other Symbols

Today's revised Catholic ritual contains numerous other symbolic objects and actions which further deepen our awareness of baptism's meaning beyond this essential note of belonging to Christ and the Trinity.

The first part of the liturgy, a *reception rite*, normally takes place at the entrance or in some similar location of the church. The celebrant meets and greets parents, godparents, and others there, then asks the children's names. He next inquires from parents and godparents if they both understand and are willing to accept the responsibility of training the youngsters in the practice of the faith.[11]

There may be two *godparents* for each child (a godfather and a godmother), but there needs to be at least one. A godparent, according to Church rules, should be mature enough to undertake the responsibility (normally 16 or over), have received the three initiation sacraments of baptism, confirmation, and the Eucharist, be an active or exemplary member of the Catholic Church, and not be the father or mother of the one to be baptized. However, a baptized and believing Christian from a separated church or community (e.g., Lutheran, Methodist, Presbyterian, etc.) may act as a Christian witness as long as there is a Catholic godparent or sponsor as well.[12]

The godparents' role is "to help the parents bring up their child to profess the faith and to show this by living it."[13]

After that dialogue with the parents and the godparents, the celebrant formally *welcomes* with great joy the children into the *Christian community* by a Sign of the Cross. To dramatize this welcoming effect of baptism, the Church encourages baptisms to be combined into a common celebration on the same day with a more substantial number of people on hand who represent the whole Church. For a similar reason the Church also insists that normally baptisms take place within the parish church and encourages occasionally, but not too often, baptism during Sunday Mass with the entire community present. [14]

The celebrant not only traces a *Sign of the Cross* on the infant's forehead but invites parents, godparents, and perhaps others as well to mark the child with this central symbol of the Christian faith. The gesture clearly reminds all that it is Jesus' cross and resurrection that has set us free, forgiven our sins, made baptism possible, given birth to the Church, and opened up the gates of the kingdom of heaven. [15]

In its ritual for the sick and the dying, the Church with reason returns to this gesture by encouraging those who care for seriously ill persons to trace a cross upon their foreheads, a reminder of the baptism which gives them hope for everlasting life.

After the reception rite, all enter the church proper for a celebration of God's Word during which participants hear appropriate biblical passages about baptism, pray for those present, call upon the saints for help, and watch as the celebrant recites an exorcism over the children.

The Church urges parents to select a *saint's name* for their children (there are thousands available, including derivatives) to provide new Christians with both models in their lives and intercessors before God.

The *exorcism*, often judged archaic in post-Vatican II days, but in more recent years deemed quite relevant with frequent experiences of the occult noted in the public media, contains phrases like these: "Cast out the power of Satan, spirit of evil," "set them free from original sin," and "send your Holy Spirit to dwell within them." The parallels drawn between the evil and Holy Spirit, between the kingdoms of darkness and light are not accidental. [16] We proclaim these new Christians for the kingdom of the Lord as opposed to the kingdom of darkness and evil.

The celebration of the Word concludes by an anointing with the *oil* of the *catechumens* on the chest of the candidate. That sacred oil, blessed by the bishop at a special Mass, thus connects this particular baptism with the diocesan shepherd and through him with the entire universal Church.

People of the Mediterranean world used oil for a variety of purposes around the time of Christ. The bodies of athletes, for example, were rubbed down with oil to make them more supple, strong, and slippery for their combat with the enemy or opponent.[17] The Church applies this meaning here immediately after the exorcism by praying that the oil of salvation given in the name of Christ the Savior will "strengthen" the children "with his power" in their future struggles against the forces of evil.[18]

Later in the ceremony the use of the *oil* of *Chrism*, likewise blessed by the bishop and spread on the crown of the person's head after the actual baptism, reflects the Jewish tradition of anointing priests, prophets, and kings and the Christian belief that Jesus was "anointed priest, prophet and king." The newly baptized is seen as sharing in those qualities through membership in Christ's Body, his holy people, the Church.[19]

The ceremony now shifts to the baptistry or the sanctuary of the church if that location offers better visibility and participation for the celebration of the sacrament. The water is blessed through a calling down of the Holy Spirit upon the water. When the water has already been blessed at Easter we instead praise God with words which recall the scriptural teachings about water, the Trinity, and the Holy Spirit mentioned above.

The celebrant then leads all present in a dialogue renunciation of sin and profession of faith.[20] *Faith*, of course, is the essential requirement for this sacrament, but infants obviously cannot express their belief, even though they may make a chorus of other sounds during the ritual. The Church, however, considers that children are baptized in the faith of the Church, which is proclaimed for them by their parents and godparents who represent both the local Church and the whole society of saints and believers.[21]

As the baptized children grow, they need subsequent formation in the faith. That kind of *Christian formation*, given primarily by the parents, seeks to lead the children "gradually to learn God's plan in Christ, so that they may ultimately accept for themselves the faith in which they have been baptized."[22]

To insure the carrying out of this crucial role of Christian formation, the Church in its introductory notes to the ritual makes very specific recommendations: the involvement of priests, religious, and lay people; visits to the family by the priest or his delegates; educational aids and sessions prior to the baptism; engagement of the family in planning and carrying out the liturgy; even the delay of baptism if there is not an assurance that the children will be given the Christian formation deemed essential.[23]

Most parishes today have developed creative baptismal preparation classes or programs, conducted in the main by dedicated lay persons, which respond to these suggestions.

In regard to the *time* of baptism, the Church states that children should be baptized within the first weeks after birth, although that period may be adjusted to allow for the mother's presence at the baptism, a gathering of several children for a common celebration, preparation for the liturgy, or the further needed Christian formation of parents. [24]

After the actual baptism, two additional rites further dramatize the effects of baptism: A *white* garment, often decorated by parents, relatives, or friends with suitable symbols and information (e.g., child's name, date of birth, day of baptism) is placed on or over the child. Now a new creation and clothed in Christ, the child wears this as an outward sign of Christian dignity to be brought unstained into the everlasting life of heaven. [25]

The paschal or Easter *candle* is located in the place of baptism and lighted throughout the ceremony. A smaller taper, also often decorated by parents, relatives, or friends, is ignited from the larger candle and presented normally to the father. The child, enlightened by Christ, is told through an admonition to the parents and godparents to keep this light burning brightly by walking as a daughter or son of Christ, the light of the world. [26]

Many priests urge parents to light this candle on the baptismal anniversary day and renew annually the promises made during the rite, eventually leading the child to respond as well. Some candle firms enclose with the box containing the baptismal candle a prayer service for home use to implement that idea.

The participants conclude the celebration by processing to the sanctuary for the recitation of the Lord's prayer and a blessing of the mother, father, and all present. Baptism as part of Christian initiation tends toward and reaches its fulfillment in the Eucharist. In a few years the baptized infant will return to the same *altar* to worship in the Spirit the Father through the Mass and receive the Son's Body and Blood in Holy Communion. The move to the altar area symbolizes this future event, but so also does the praying together of the Our Father. The Church always has and continues today to use this ancient formula as a ritual preparation for Communion. The words "daily bread" take on a meaning beyond the human food we require and point to the divine nourishment we will soon eat and drink.

Moreover, the baptized infants, now daughters and sons of the Father, sisters and brothers of Christ, with the Holy Spirit dwelling inside them, can more fittingly through the parents, godparents, and others present speak to their God with such intimate terms.

Institution by Christ

At first glance the Gospels seem to give us explicit words of Christ establishing the sacrament of baptism. To the Pharisee named Nicodemus who came to Jesus at night, the Lord said:

> "No one can enter into God's kingdom
> without being begotten of water and Spirit" (John 3:5).

Even more direct would be the risen Lord's command:

> "Go into the whole world and proclaim the good news to all creation. The man who believes in it and accepts baptism will be saved; the man who refuses to believe in it will be condemned" (Mark 16:15-16).

As we have seen, at the end of Matthew's Gospel the resurrected Christ likewise commissioned the eleven apostles (Judas had taken his life and a successor had not yet been appointed) to make disciples of all nations and baptize in the name of the Trinity (Matt 28:16-19).

Scripture scholars in our time, however, raise serious questions about the historical accuracy of these texts—whether they were the actual words of Jesus or rather the early Church's profession of faith in Christ and its understanding of him. [27] Theologians thus look instead for information about baptism's institution to what they term the narrative texts in the Acts of the Apostles. These describe the actual practice and experience of baptism or Christian initiation in the early Church. We listed those major events from the Acts in a previous context. [28]

The same students of baptism then turn to St. Paul's writings for a deeper understanding, for the theology, and for the doctrine of the early Church about this sacrament. [29] The classic passage cited is in his Letter to the Romans (6:3-11), where the great Apostle compares the death and resurrection of baptism to Jesus' dying and rising:

> Are you not aware that we who were baptized into Christ Jesus were baptized into his death? Through baptism into his death we were buried with him, so that, just as Christ was raised from the dead by the glory of the Father, we too might live a new life. If we have

been united with him through likeness to his death, so shall we be through a like resurrection. (6:3-5).

The baptismal font in Rome at the major Basilica of St. Paul's Outside the Walls reflects this text. Steps lead down into and up out of a pool. Those words from Romans are inscribed in mosaic letters high on the four walls surrounding that font in the baptistry.

Whether or not Jesus gave a direct command to baptize and thus how he instituted the sacrament is still a debate among scholars. But all agree that Jesus, by his life and Easter victory, commanded his Church to preach the Gospel, make converts, and initiate them into the community. Baptism, therefore, directly or indirectly comes from Christ the Lord. [30]

The Effects of Baptism

Baptism opens the door to eternal life for believers, ushers them into the kingdom of God, incorporates them into the Church, cleanses them from sin, makes them sharers in God's own life, and transforms them into God's adopted children. [31] Baptism, however, is not an isolated event or a totally separate sacrament. It starts a person on a journey. It stands as the first formal step of initiation into the Christian life. It should be complemented by confirmation and reach fulfillment on earth in the Eucharist and after death in a face-to-face meeting with God.

The Church, quite succinctly but with these carefully chosen, rich words, describes the effects of the Christian initiation process, of which baptism is a key and integral element:

> Through the sacraments of Christian initiation men and women are freed from the power of darkness. With Christ they die, are buried and rise again. They receive the Spirit of adoption which makes them God's sons and daughters and, with the entire people of God, they celebrate the memorial of the Lord's death and resurrection.
>
> Through baptism men and women are incorporated into Christ. They are formed into God's people, and they obtain forgiveness of all their sins. They are raised from their natural human condition to the dignity of adopted children. They become a new creation through water and the Holy Spirit. Hence they are called, and are indeed, the children of God.
>
> Signed with the gift of the Spirit in confirmation, Christians more perfectly become the image of their Lord and are filled with the Holy Spirit. They bear witness to him before all the world and eagerly work for the building up of the body of Christ.

Finally they come to the table of the eucharist, to eat the flesh and drink the blood of the Son of Man so that they may have eternal life and show forth the unity of God's people. By offering themselves with Christ, they share in his universal sacrifice: the entire community of the redeemed is offered to God by their high priest. They pray for a greater outpouring of the Holy Spirit so that the whole human race may be brought into the unity of God's family.

Thus the three sacraments of Christian initiation closely combine to bring the faithful to the full stature of Christ and to enable them to carry out the mission of the entire people of God in the Church and in the world. [32]

Baptism is the foundational and pivotal sacrament of the Catholic Christian life.

Discussion Questions

1. Why is Easter the most important celebration in the Church year, more significant, for example, even than Christmas?
2. Reread the first section of this chapter and list the various stages of the Rite of Christian Initiation of Adults.
3. Can you give an explanation for the Church's insistence that ordinarily baptism be celebrated on Sunday?
4. What is the essential part of the baptismal rite?
5. Identify some incidents in which you have experienced the positive life-giving effects of water and some in which you have witnessed the destructive, death-dealing impact of water.
6. Take out your Bible and look up the scriptural readings mentioning water noted in the early section of this chapter under "water."
7. Explain the meaning of being baptized "In the name of . . . ."
8. What are the requirements for the godparents and/or Christian witness of one about to be baptized?
9. Discuss the meaning of these symbols and gestures in the baptism liturgy: Sign of the Cross, saint's name, exorcism, oil of catechumens, oil of chrism, white garment, candle, the Our Father.
10. Is baptism a once-only event or part of a process? What are its effects?

CONFIRMATION:

a gift
of the
Spirit

3

Confirmation: Gift of the Spirit

The Church ordinarily confirms adults and youth in different ways. Adults normally receive confirmation when they enter the Catholic Church according to the Rite of Christian Initiation of Adults. As we have seen, that combined baptism/confirmation/Eucharist ritual usually occurs during the Easter vigil service because of its close connection with the paschal or passover mystery of Jesus' death and resurrection.

Youth in the United States today, on the other hand, most often receive this sacrament during their mid-teen years. They prepare for the celebration by a lengthy, two-or-three year process of guided study, spiritual renewal, and service projects. Then on a date agreed upon with diocesan officials the candidates gather with sponsors, relatives, and friends for a unique solemn ceremony, generally in the context of a Mass, during which the bishop confirms them.

The presence of the bishop, either in person or at least through the fact that he blessed the chrism oil spread over the person's forehead, is key to the meaning of the ceremony and sacrament. As a successor to the original apostles, the bishop links this particular confirmation with the original outpouring of the Spirit on the first Pentecost described in the Acts of the Apostles, chapter 2:

> When the day of Pentecost came it found them gathered in one place. Suddenly from up in the sky there came a noise like a strong, driving wind which was heard all through the house where they were seated. Tongues as of fire appeared, which parted and came to rest

on each of them. All were filled with the Holy Spirit. They began to express themselves in foreign tongues and make bold proclamation as the Spirit prompted them. (2:1-4).

As a brother to other bishops throughout the world, including the pope, the bishop symbolizes the wider Church to which the confirmed belong and for the service of which they have been called through this sacrament. Pope Paul VI, the bishop of Rome, noted this dimension of confirmation when he issued the revised ritual in 1971. "Moreover, having received the character of this sacrament, they are 'bound more intimately to the Church' and 'they are more strictly obliged to spread and defend the faith both by word and by deed as true witnesses of Christ.'"[1]

Baptism, Confirmation, and the Eucharist

The rite of confirmation has followed a diverse and complicated course in the history of the Church. At first simply part of initiation and only later a separate ceremony, it has nevertheless always been seen as a complement to baptism, leading to fulfillment in the Eucharist. To show these connected relationships, the Church prefers to celebrate the sacrament within Mass although allowing other possibilities outside of Mass. Thus, when confirmation is celebrated within Mass, non-baptized adults who seek admission to the Church are first baptized, then confirmed by the bishop or priest and, finally, given for the initial time the Lord's Body and Blood. For an adult previously baptized in another tradition, there is no re-baptism, but the rest of the rite remains the same.

For the younger person, who probably has already been baptized and made First Communion, confirmation within Mass after the homily manifests at least on this occasion the baptism/confirmation/Eucharist order of initiation.

Our discussion below on the details of the celebration will examine the confirmation ceremony separate from the Rite of Christian Initiation of Adults. As we observed about baptism in the preceding chapter, these elements hold true, with adaptations, for both the adult and youth rituals of confirmation.

Scriptural Readings

Whether confirmation is celebrated within or outside of Mass, the Church always insists upon a Liturgy of the Word before ministering the actual sacrament. In urging that a suitable emphasis be given to this biblical proclamation, the introduction to confirmation offers reasons for such a stress upon the Scriptures: "It is from the hearing of the word of God that the many-sided power of the Holy Spirit flows upon the Church and upon each one of the baptized and confirmed, and it is by this word that God's will is manifest in the life of Christians."[2]

The lectionary of scriptural texts developed after the Second Vatican Council and used for the Eucharist and other liturgical celebrations contains a wealth of texts which bear a connection to confirmation.

There are five Old Testament selections, including familiar passages from the prophets Isaiah, Ezekiel, and Joel. For example, "I will give you a new heart and place a new spirit within you . . . ." (Ezek 36:24).

There are a dozen New Testament selections, including the account of Pentecost from Acts 2 and several passages from Paul which give more of a theology about the Holy Spirit. For example, "The Spirit too helps us in our weakness, for we do not know how to pray as we ought . . . ." (Rom 8:26).

After a half dozen responsorial psalms and alleluia verses, there are twelve gospel excerpts, including Jesus' frequent promises that he would send his Spirit upon believers. For example:

> If you love me
> and obey the commands I give you,
> I will ask the Father
> and he will give you another Paraclete—
> to be with you always:
> the Spirit of truth,
> whom the world cannot accept . . . (John 14:15-17).

Laying-on of Hands

The bishop or another person preaches a suitable homily after the biblical readings and then all present, including the candidates, renew their baptismal promises, thereby making very explicit the connection between baptism and confirmation.

The priests participating at this point of the celebration assemble on either side of the bishop and with him "lay hands upon all the candidates (by extending their hands over them)."[3]

The laying-on of hands gesture is rich in meaning. First, it recalls two incidents, among others, in the Acts of the Apostles during which Peter and John as well as Paul laid hands upon new members of the Church, and through this action the recipients received the Holy Spirit:

> Peter and John . . . went down to these people and prayed that they might receive the Holy Spirit. It had not as yet come down upon any of them since they had only been baptized in the name of the Lord Jesus. The pair upon arriving imposed hands on them and they received the Holy Spirit (8:14-17).

> When they heard this, they were baptized in the name of the Lord Jesus. As Paul laid his hands on them, the Holy Spirit came down on them and they began to speak in tongues and to utter prophecies (19:5-6).

Second, it reminds us that among the fundamental or initial elements of Christian teaching in the early Church as sketched in the Letter to the Hebrews were "instruction about baptism and laying-on of hands" (6:2).[4]

Third, it follows the pattern of all the revised liturgical rites in which there has been restored some form of this laying-on of hands. We will describe in our discussion of holy orders and anointing of the sick how those rituals very explicitly call for that gesture; the other sacraments also require the laying-on of hands, but in less definitive ways, like the signing with the cross, anointing with chrism, and final blessing in baptism.

Fourth, the laying-on of hands possesses an ancient history of deep significance both in and outside of the Judeo-Christian heritage. This action symbolizes according to that tradition the setting aside of a person for a special function, bestowal of power, initiation into a community, restoration or reconciliation of an alienated member, transmission of grace, and the healing touch of Christ.

Gifts of the Spirit

The laying-on of hands gesture is accompanied by the bishop's singing or saying a prayer for the outpouring of the Holy Spirit upon the candidates. While these words and actions are not essential, they nevertheless should be emphasized to bring out the complete effect of the rite and facilitate a fuller understanding of the sacrament's meaning.[5]

The prayer itself connects confirmation with baptism and asks for the seven gifts of the Holy Spirit:

> All-powerful God, Father of our Lord Jesus Christ,
> by water and the Holy Spirit

you freed your sons and daughters from sin
and gave them new life.
Send your Holy Spirit upon them
to be their Helper and Guide.
Give them the spirit of wisdom and understanding,
the spirit of right judgment and courage,
the spirit of knowledge and reverence.
Fill them with the spirit of wonder and awe in your presence. [6]

Anointing with Chrism

Immediately prior to the Second Vatican Council and for some seven centuries before that confirmation in the Latin rite or the West was administered by tracing with the oil of chrism a cross on the forehead of the candidate and reciting the words, "I sign you with the sign of the cross and confirm you with the chrism of salvation. In the name of the Father and of the Son and of the Holy Spirit." The significance of that chrism was described in the previous chapter on baptism.

When Pope Paul VI issued the restored ritual in 1971, however, he outlined the complex history of confirmation, changed the formula, and specified the essential elements for the sacrament's celebration today. "The Sacrament of Confirmation is conferred through the anointing with chrism on the forehead, which is done by the laying-on of the hand, and through the words: 'N., be sealed with the gift of the Holy Spirit.' "[7]

While acknowledging the validity and suitability of the earlier formula, Pope Paul VI indicated that he judged preferable the very ancient formula of the Byzantine rite or the East "by which the gift of the Holy Spirit himself is expressed and the outpouring of the Spirit which took place on the day of Pentecost is recalled (Acts 2:1–4, 38)."[8]

Sponsors

The bishop, as we observed, is the original and ordinary minister of confirmation. His presence recalls the first outpouring upon the apostles at Pentecost, the close bond forged between the confirmed and the Church, as well as the obligation henceforth for the confirmed to be witnesses of Christ to others in the world. The bishop may, however, associate other priests with himself in the administration of this sacrament. [9]

The candidate receives the promise of further unique support for that task at this moment through the presence of a sponsor or sponsors during the anointing ritual. Each candidate must have one and may have two sponsors who ideally should be the same persons as the godparents for baptism, thus manifesting the link between those sacraments. However, the Church also allows a special sponsor for confirmation. Although parents may not assume that role, they may present their son or daughter for the sacrament. [10]

The requirements for a confirmation sponsor are basically the same as those requisites for a baptism godparent: spiritually qualified, sufficiently mature, a member of the Catholic Church, and a person initiated in the sacraments of baptism, confirmation, and the Eucharist. [11]

Sponsors place their right hands upon the candidate's shoulder during the actual confirmation and give the candidate's name to the bishop unless the candidate announces her or his own name. The name would be the baptismal name plus perhaps an additional saint's name selected in the latter case by the candidate specifically for confirmation. The candidate thereby seeks another model and heavenly intercessor as she or he continues the Christian journey. [12]

Our Father

After celebration of the sacrament itself, the community prays for the newly confirmed, their parents and godparents, leaders of the Church, and others throughout the world. Since confirmation normally takes place in the context of a Mass, the rite then moves to the Liturgy of the Eucharist. The Church attaches particular value to the saying of the Our Father prior to Communion, not only because of that prayer's relationship to communion, as we mentioned in the discussion on baptism, but also "because it is the Spirit who prays in us, and in the Spirit the Christian says 'Abba, Father.' "[13]

Confirmation's Origin

In the contemporary Latin or western rite of the Roman Catholic Church, we celebrate the sacrament of confirmation as a separate and distinct ceremony, even though intimately linked to baptism. But such has not always been the case. In fact, confirmation did not even exist as a separate ritual on its own until the third century, and that distinct rite became a regular practice only after the fifth century. Moreover, it was the Middle Ages before confirmation became definitely separated from baptismal initiation, was named among the seven official sacraments, and did receive a separate theological justification. [14]

Jesus' promises to send the Holy Spirit are frequent and explicit in the Gospels. In addition, the Acts cite many references to an outpouring of the Spirit upon early Christians. It is difficult, however, to determine at what precise liturgical rite that did occur.

The passages from the Acts of the Apostles which we recalled earlier described Peter, John, and Paul performing a rite with the laying-on of hands that brought forth the Holy Spirit upon the recipients. However, most current scholars, examining those texts in detail, conclude that these refer to the total baptismal initiation rite and not to a special confirmation ritual. [15]

The subsequent history and development of confirmation in the Church is unclear and confusing. A respected historian thus summarizes the situation during the first four centuries in this way: there was no common consensus about the point at which people received the Holy Spirit during their initiation as Christians. All agreed that by the conclusion of the ceremony Christians had received the Spirit, but for some this occurred during the baptismal washing, for others it happened afterwards. [16]

As time went on the separation in practice between baptism and confirmation began and for various reasons grew deeper and wider. Then theologians started to reflect upon the procedures and propose reasons for the separate approach, seeing baptism as a sacrament for forgiveness and confirmation as a sacrament for strengthening. [17]

In our day, while the separateness in celebration of the two sacraments continues to exist, confirmation is viewed more as a complement, a fulfillment, a completion of the work begun in baptism. [18]

Effects of Confirmation

The official ritual succinctly states the powerful effects of confirmation:

> Those who have been baptized continue on the path of Christian initiation through the sacrament of confirmation. In this sacrament they receive the Holy Spirit, who was sent upon the apostles by the Lord on Pentecost.
>
> This giving of the Holy Spirit conforms believers more perfectly to Christ and strengthens them so that they may bear witness to Christ for the building up of his body in faith and love. They are so marked

with the character or seal of the Lord that the sacrament of confirmation cannot be repeated. [19]

The *seven gifts*, asked for in the prayer before the anointing, merely specify the assistance promised by Christ through the action of the Holy Spirit. Wisdom, understanding, right judgment, courage, knowledge, reverence, and wonder or awe in God's presence provide us with guidance to discern and strength to follow the Lord's path in our lives. The Holy Spirit indeed becomes our helper and guide.

In a sense we might term these personal gifts helping us as individuals to grow in our relationship with the Father. St. Paul, in his First Letter to the Corinthians, speaks of other powers bestowed by the Spirit upon believers which might be called in contrast social gifts since their purpose is to build up the Church, the Body of Christ. These *charisms* include wisdom in discourse, the power to express knowledge, the gift of healing, miraculous powers, prophecy, the power to distinguish one spirit from another, the gift of tongues, and the ability to interpret tongues. To each person such a "manifestation of the Spirit is given for the common good" (1 Cor 12:4-11).

The confirmation ritual summarizes the impact of this sacrament upon the recipient:

> The anointing with chrism and the accompanying words express clearly the effects of the giving of the Holy Spirit. Signed with the perfumed oil, the baptized person receives the indelible character, the seal of the Lord, together with the gift of the Spirit, which conforms him more closely to Christ and gives him the grace of spreading the Lord's presence among men. [20]

Living more closely in conformity with Christ and attempting to spread the Lord's presence among all people, will result in what St. Paul and the Church term the *fruits of the Holy Spirit:* "Love, joy, peace, patient endurance, kindness, generosity, faith, mildness, and chastity." These stand in opposition to the works of the flesh: "lewd conduct, impurity, licentiousness, idolatry, sorcery, hostilities, bickering, jealousy, outbursts of rage, selfish rivalries, dissensions, factions, envy, drunkenness, orgies and the like." [21]

Baptism in the Spirit

Since the 1960s in the United States and elsewhere many Roman Catholics have spoken and do speak about being baptized in the Holy Spirit. They normally mean by this neither the ritual washing and words of sacramental baptism nor the gift of the Holy Spirit in the sacrament of confirmation. Instead, they refer to a deep, personal experience of the Holy Spirit which has transformed their lives.

This awakening of the Spirit within them usually occurs during a series of prayerful, reflective learning sessions called "Life in the Spirit" or "Friendship with Jesus" seminars and not within a specifically sacramental celebration. Participants pray for this baptism in the Spirit and for the gift of praying in tongues. Significant transformations in people's lives often occur and foster these characteristics within them:

- an active belief in the Holy Spirit's working presence today
- a personal relationship with the Lord Jesus
- a great love for Scripture
- an ease with and desire for spontaneous, enthusiastic community
- externalized prayer
- a love for religious singing
- the ability to pray in tongues
- a phenomenon known as "resting in the Spirit"
- and an acceptance of prophecy as St. Paul described that gift.

Moreover, many have as a result returned to the sacramental life of the Church and become more active members of their parishes.

Some of the charismatic renewal leaders would prefer the term "release," "outpouring", or "awakening" of the Holy Spirit to describe this experience rather than baptism lest it seem to deny the truth that the baptized-confirmed person has already received the Holy Spirit in those initiation sacraments. [22]

Conclusion

By baptism we enter into fellowship with the Father, the Son, and the Holy Spirit. [23] That Holy Spirit becomes further present to us in a unique way through the sacrament of confirmation. Both, however, point toward and prepare us for the Eucharist which completes the initiation process and is its fulfillment.

Discussion Questions

1. When was the Holy Spirit first given to early Christians and what happened on that occasion?
2. List the three sacraments of initiation and the order in which they should be received.

3. Secure a copy of the lectionary and note the readings provided for the sacrament of confirmation.*

4. Can you identify the "laying-on of hands" gesture in each of the seven sacraments? Why does the Church see this as so significant an action?

5. What are the essential elements in the rite of confirmation today?

6. Who would you recommend as a suitable sponsor for someone about to be confirmed?

7. Write down the seven gifts of the Holy Spirit and reflect upon a few recent occasions when these effects of confirmation did or could have helped you make the right decision and carry it out despite difficulties entailed.

8. The Church today urges all baptized/confirmed members to use their unique talents or charisms to build up the Church and make the world a better place in which to live. Think of people carrying out this charge, like readers in Church or visitors to the sick, and list as many different functions as you can.

9. The Holy Spirit produces certain fruits in people's lives: love, joy, peace, patient endurance, kindness, generosity, faith, mildness, and chastity. Can you identify five persons you know or know about who seem to reflect those fruits or one of them in their lives?

10. Does any acquaintance of yours claim to be a charismatic and to have been baptized in the Spirit? Ask her or him what those words mean and to describe how charismatics pray.

*Confirmation: Official Rite is available from The Liturgical Press, Collegeville, Minnesota.

THE EUCHARIST:

worship,
food,
and
presence

4

The Eucharist: Worship, Food, and Presence

A crystal prism hangs suspended from the ceiling next to the window in the office of the Renew director for the Syracuse Diocese. On a clear day the sun's rays, striking that gently revolving object, reflect around the room in a constantly shifting variety of magnificent colors.

In somewhat similar fashion, when a couple in love examine an engagement ring, they turn the diamond about and gaze at it from several different angles to discover in better fashion the beauty of that jewel.

When the prism remains fixed in one position or we look at the diamond from only a single vantage point, we fail to catch the full richness of both realities. Similarly when encountering one of the Church's mysteries, we need, so to speak, to turn it around and examine it from different perspectives for a fuller appreciation of the mystery. Even then, however, we can never totally exhaust its depths because of the divine element contained within each mystery.

The Eucharist illustrates that principle. It is at one and the same time: the most perfect sacrificial worship of the Father through Christ in the Spirit which humans can offer; the Body and Blood of Jesus given to us as spiritual food; the risen Lord substantially and permanently present under the elements of bread and wine for our adoration.[1]

To omit from consideration any of these aspects of the Eucharist gives us an inadequate understanding and appreciation of this sublime sacrament. To concentrate or, as it were, overemphasize a single dimension of the Eucharist, tends to give us a distorted notion of the sacrament. To examine all three elements provides us with a better awareness of this ineffable mystery.

The revised and current code of canon law expresses that teaching and its practical consequences for Catholics: "The Most Holy Eucharist is the most august sacrament, in which Christ the Lord himself is contained, offered and received, and by which the Church constantly lives and grows." "The faithful are to hold the Eucharist in highest honor, taking part in the celebration of the Most August Sacrifice, receiving the sacrament devoutly and frequently, and worshiping it with supreme adoration."[2]

We will consider the Eucharist, briefly because of space limitations, in those three ways—as worship, food, and presence.

The Eucharist as Worship

Early Beginnings

St. Paul wrote his first letter to the Christians living at Corinth around the year A.D. 57. In two chapters of that epistle (1 Cor 10–11), we have the earliest written record of Jesus' Last Supper on Holy Thursday and of the early Christians' subsequent celebrations of the Lord's Supper. While addressing certain abuses connected with the meal surrounding this worship experience, Paul recalled what happened at that first Eucharist:

> I received from the Lord what I handed on to you, namely, that the Lord Jesus on the night in which he was betrayed took bread, and after he had given thanks, broke it and said, "This is my body, which is for you. Do this in remembrance of me." In the same way, after the supper, he took the cup, saying, "This cup is the new covenant in my blood. Do this, whenever you drink it, in remembrance of me." Every time, then, you eat this bread and drink this cup, you proclaim the death of the Lord until he comes! This means that whoever eats the bread or drinks the cup of the Lord unworthily sins against the body and blood of the Lord (1 Cor 11:23-27).

Later, between the years A.D. 60–80, the three Gospel narratives of the Last Supper appeared (Matt 26:26-29; Mark 14:22-25; Luke 22:14-20). Because of the brevity and ambiguity in these four accounts, biblical scholars disagree about the precise meaning of the institutional narrative. Was the Eucharistic bread and wine mentioned understood as being Christ's Body and Blood really or only symbolically?[3]

'Later yet, but still very early in the Church's history, around A.D. 90, the Fourth Gospel spends five chapters on the Last Supper, but never mentions the bread and wine or Jesus' words over them (John 13–17). However, in chapter 6 the author of John's Gospel seems to communicate his understanding of the Eucharist. In a lengthy passage on the bread of life, Jesus is quoted as saying among other things:

> I myself am the bread of life.
> . . . For my flesh is real food
> and my blood real drink.
> The man who feeds on my flesh
> and drinks my blood
> remains in me, and I in him" (6:35; 55-56).

While there is some dispute among Scripture scholars about the precise meaning of John's words as well, it seems certain that most Christians within a century or so of Jesus' death did take the words of the Last Supper literally, believed Christ's Body and Blood was really present under the sign of bread and wine, and considered as heretics those who did not so believe.[4]

At the same time, Christians began more clearly to view the Eucharist as a sacrificial meal. They saw Jesus as the Messiah, the crucifixion as a sacrificial death of Christ offering himself to the Father, and the Last Supper as an unbloody commemoration of the Lord's passion and his victory over death. The consequence of those beliefs made the Eucharist into a sacrificial meal or banquet through which participants continue and share in the sacrifice of Christ.[5] The Letter to the Hebrews develops these notions at length (4:14–10:31).

A Developing Judeo-Christian Service

Most of the initial Christians were Jewish converts. Quite understandably, therefore, the first ways of worshipping followed the pattern of Jewish practices or actually fused them with the specifically Christian Eucharist. Thus, the passover celebration as the context from which the Last Supper developed, the events of the Old Testament or Hebrew Scriptures during which God intervened to save the Chosen People, and the daily or weekly synagogue prayer services—all of these elements had their influence on Christian worship and can be detected even today in the most recent form of the

Roman Catholic Eucharistic service published after the Second Vatican Council.

This excerpt from the Acts of the Apostles captures the spirit and practice of the early Church, including the style of worship:

> They devoted themselves to the apostles' instruction and the communal life, to the breaking of bread and the prayers. A reverent fear overtook them all, for many wonders and signs were performed by the apostles. Those who believed shared all things in common; they would sell their property and goods, dividing everything on the basis of each one's need. They went to the temple area together every day, while in their homes they broke bread. With exultant and sincere hearts they took their meals in common, praising God and winning the approval of all the people. Day by day the Lord added to their number those who were being saved (2:42-47).

A More Specifically Christian Eucharist

Soon the regular day for Christian worship shifted to the day of the Sun as opposed to the Saturday observation of the sabbath, partially because the great Christian events—Easter and Pentecost—occurred on Sunday.

For the first three centuries the Church suffered persecutions, sometimes from Jewish antagonists and sometimes from secular authorities. That opposition, among other factors, kept the Eucharistic celebrations relatively simple, comparatively brief, usually in small groups, often at homes, sometimes secret, presided over by bishops or, later, priests and offered in the common language of Greek with the people actively involved in various ways.

Church Growth and Liturgical Change

When the edict of Constantine in 313 lifted the legal ban on Christian worship, the Church came forth from its hiding places. Thereafter, with the rapid growth of Christianity, the construction of basilicas or large churches and the influence of the imperial culture upon the Eucharistic celebrations, the service became an elaborate, rich ceremonial liturgy now offered in the new native language of Latin.[6]

During the Middle Ages the celebration of the Eucharist gradually came to be more clergy dominated. The laity were less actively involved, received Communion infrequently, and found the Latin more difficult to understand. The sacrificial and real presence dimensions of the Eucharist were stressed and the spiritual food, meal, or Communion element underplayed. For example, the small white wafer used for the consecrated bread came to be known as a "host" from the Latin word for a sacrificial victim.[7] Ultimately, because of such trends the Church even found it necessary to require Catholics by law to receive Communion at least once a year during a specified period, a practice known in more recent times as making one's "Easter duty."

Protestant Reformation and Council of Trent

Over the years prior to the Protestant reformation of the sixteenth century, certain abuses had crept into Catholic worship, and a great diversity of rituals had emerged. The Council of Trent sought to correct those conditions, and as a result of its efforts Pope Pius V in 1570 published a Roman Missal which was to be the official ritual book followed in Catholic churches for the next four hundred years. The Last Supper liturgy, generally called by the Greek word *Eucharist*, which means "thanksgiving," also came to be termed the *Mass* from the Latin concluding word of the ritual which means "being sent forth."

While the Roman Missal of 1570 brought unity to the Eucharistic celebrations and encouraged the laity to receive Communion regularly, in general the Mass continued to be a service heavily dominated by the clergy, with the people as mute observers or silent spectators.

Contemporary Liturgical Revisions

Around the beginning of the twentieth century, a movement from below and decisions from above gradually changed the Eucharistic ritual, recovering the best traditions of the earliest Christian years and restoring the lay people to active participation. Those efforts culminated in the Constitution on the Sacred Liturgy promulgated by the Second Vatican Council in 1963. That broad document called for a total revision of all the liturgical books, including the Roman Missal and the ritual for every sacrament. The extensive, inter-disciplinary effort to achieve this momentous task took more than a decade, and in 1970 a new Roman Missal was issued by Pope Paul VI with other rites published subsequently.

The Catholic Mass of today, which includes such elements as liturgy in the vernacular language, active congregational participation, a variety of ministerial roles by lay persons (readers, Eucharistic ministers, leaders of song, greeters, gift bearers), and a large majority receiving Communion even under the appearance of both bread and wine reflects the fruit of that double effort of liturgical revision from the grass roots and by the official Church.[8]

The General Instruction or Introduction to the Revised Roman Missal summarizes the Church's view today of the Eucharist as worship:

> At Mass or the Lord's Supper, the people of God are called together, with a priest presiding and acting in the person of Christ, to celebrate the memorial of the Lord or eucharistic sacrifice. For this reason Christ's promise applies supremely to such a local gathering together of the Church: "Where two or three come together in my name, there am I in their midst" (Mt 18:20). For at the celebration of Mass, which perpetuates the sacrifice of the cross, Christ is really present to the assembly gathered in his name; he is present in the person of the minister, in his own word, and indeed substantially and permanently under the eucharistic elements.[9]

The same document in its next paragraph summarizes the general structure of the Eucharistic celebration:

> The Mass is made up as it were of the liturgy of the word and the liturgy of the eucharist, two parts so closely connected that they form but one single act of worship. For in the Mass the table of God's word and of Christ's body is laid for the people of God to receive from it instruction and food. There are also certain rites to open and conclude the celebration.[10]

The Mass as seen today consists, therefore, in a brief gathering rite, a Liturgy of the Word which centers around the pulpit or the lectern with the reading and proclaiming of the Scriptures, a liturgy of the Eucharist which centers around the altar with preparation, consecration, and communion of the gifts, and a short dismissal rite.

The Eucharist as Food

As we have noted the Eucharist is also the Body and Blood of Jesus given to us as spiritual food which we are to receive as a sacrament devoutly and frequently.

History of Communion Practices

The literal and obvious meaning of Jesus' words at the Last Supper, "Take and eat . . . . Take and drink . . . ." is that those who participate in the sacrificial meal of the Mass will communicate during the Eucharistic celebration. Such in fact was the tradition of Catholic Christians in the first centuries of the Church. Moreover, not only did they receive Christ's Body regularly under the sign of bread, but also drank the Lord's Blood from the cup under the sign of wine.

At the same time, the faithful on occasion did communicate under one kind or species only. Since daily Mass was an infrequent practice in the very early Church, Christians would take the consecrated bread home and communicate themselves during the week. They also carried the Eucharist in that fashion to the sick, prisoners, or to monks living in isolation. In addition, Communion under the sign of wine only for people unable to consume the consecrated bread, for example, infants and the gravely ill, formed a standard custom in those years. Even then Christians recognized that each kind, blessed bread or wine, contained the whole Christ, present Body and Blood, soul and divinity, in all the fullness and power of his life, sufferings, and resurrection.

Practical difficulties and poor attitudes combined to produce a change in the thirteenth and fourteenth centuries. The faithful, as we have noted, for complicated historical reasons approached Communion much less frequently and, unfortunately, failed to realize that the sacrifice and sacrificial meal are one in the Mass. There likewise was a deeper and clearer understanding that the entire Christ is present under either the consecrated bread or wine and in every particle or portion of the blessed species.

These doctrinal and devotional attitudes, combined with contagion in times of rampant diseases, the possibility of irreverence or spilling, the hesitation of some communicants to drink from the common cup, the large numbers at Easter and other special feasts, and the scarcity of wine in northern countries, led to a gradual abandonment of Communion under both kinds.

A reaction set in during the fourteenth century and ultimately many reformers urged a return to the early Christian tradition. Still, in doing so some maintained that Communion under the sign of bread alone was invalid, a deprivation, an incomplete and erroneous fulfillment of the Lord's teaching in John's Gospel. Roman Catholics reacted in the face of those attacks and discouraged or forbade reintroduction of the practice under such doctrinal conditions.

The Second Vatican Council decreed the restoration of Communion under both kinds for the laity on occasions when this would be pastorally useful. Still, in doing so, the Church insisted on appropriate instruction for the faithful so they would understand that no grace necessary for salvation is lost should they receive under one form only. Nevertheless, just as article 55 in the Constitution on the Sacred Liturgy taught that the most perfect form of participation in the Mass was for the faithful to receive the Lord's Body from the same sacrifice, so, too, the Church views communion under both kinds as a fuller sign of carrying out Jesus' command at the Last Supper.

In the United States Communion under both kinds has been gradually introduced with generally positive reactions. Today there is official approval of this practice for almost all occasions if the local pastoral leadership judges it would be feasible and beneficial. [11]

Preparation for Communion

To insure that we approach Communion with the proper understanding and motivation, the Church requires three elements in preparation: appropriate knowledge, fasting from food, and freedom from serious sinfulness.

Those who enter the Church as adults naturally will study the Eucharist in detail as part of their formation program. Children, on the other hand, usually in the early years of elementary school, gain the necessary understanding through a course of instruction. This "First Communion Program" primarily involves the pastor and the parents, but may also engage the Catholic school instructors or religious education teachers. When "they have sufficient knowledge . . . so as to understand the mystery of Christ according to their capacity and can receive the Body of the Lord with faith and devotion," the young boys and girls, generally between six and eight, make their initial communion with their families and/or as a class [12]

Older Catholics can relate classical stories of both the Lenten and Communion rules for fasting. Lent until two decades ago was a time for meatless meals, no snacks, and hot cross buns. To receive Communion required abstaining from food or drink, including water, from midnight until after Mass. Such a fasting preparation for major spiritual events (e.g., Easter and Communion) has an ancient history in the Church and even in Jewish as well as other religious traditions. Its value for disposing the human heart has been clearly established by centuries of experience and modern psychological research.

Nevertheless, contemporary circumstances led the Church gradually to mitigate regulations for both the Lenten and Communion fasts. It continues to encourage voluntary fasting of various sorts, including from food and drink, but requires only a minimal amount. In the case of Communion, one is "to abstain from any food or drink, with the exception only of water and medicine, for at least the period of one hour before Holy Communion."[13]

Sitting down at table with someone normally is a sign of closeness, oneness, and harmony. It would be inconsistent, therefore, to eat the Lord's Body and Blood when we are in a state or condition of serious sinfulness which, by definition, breaks our friendship or relationship with Christ and fellow Christians. The Church thus states:

> A person who is conscious of grave sin is not to celebrate Mass or to receive the Body of the Lord without prior sacramental confession unless a grave reason is present and there is no opportunity for confessing; in this case the person is to be mindful of the obligation to make an act of perfect contrition, including the intention of confessing as soon as possible.[14]

Programs of preparation for the reception of penance by children usually occur somewhat around the same time as those for the Eucharist. Normally, these likewise actively involve the parents who with the parish priest determine the precise occasion when their son or daughter is "correctly prepared" and ready for both sacraments.[15]

Grace of Communion

Baptism and confirmation, the other two sacraments of the initiation process, communicate a permanent character to the recipients and are never repeated. The Eucharist, however, may be received often, even daily. The faithful, as cited earlier, have an obligation to receive Communion at least once a year, normally during the Easter season.[16] Catholics may receive also more than once a day, but only when the Eucharists at which they participate have a special significance.[17]

In all of the other sacraments, the person receives the grace of Christ; in Holy Communion, the person receives Christ himself. For this reason the Church has always considered the Eucharist as the center, the heart, and the summit of its life. It is the most perfect worship of the Father we can give, but also the most perfect gift of God we can receive.

St. Thomas Aquinas, the great medieval doctor of the Church, in one succinct but profound sentence, summarized the effects of

Holy Communion upon us: "This sacrament does for the spiritual life all that natural food does for the bodily life, namely, by sustaining, giving increase, restoring and giving delight."[18]

Receiving Jesus in Communion, consequently, sustains us in the Christian life, increases our sharing in the risen Lord's life within us, forgives our sins or brings us back closer to Christ, and produces a deep spiritual joy in our hearts.

The Church is anxious that those who are confined to homes, health care centers, or hospitals should have the opportunity frequently, even daily to receive Communion. We will discuss that situation in chapter 6 on the sacrament of anointing the sick.

The Eucharist as Presence

History of This Devotion

We saw at the beginning of this chapter that within a century of Jesus' death and resurrection, most Christians believed that the Lord's Body and Blood was truly present under the sign of bread and wine. They also believed in his on-going presence after the completion of the Eucharistic celebration, preserving the consecrated bread especially for self-communion during the week or for Communion to the sick.

However, formal devotion to the real presence came at a later time, during the Middle Ages, and as might be expected, for a diversity of complex reasons. Perhaps the most significant factor was the shift from a liturgy in which people fully participated to a worship dominated by the clergy. The faithful understood less (Latin no longer was the common person's language) of what was happening and their role became more that of passive participant. In addition, and accompanying all this, was an emphasis on the dignity and awesomeness of the divine presence in the Eucharist with a consequent reduction in appreciation for the Eucharist as our spiritual food.

The devotional life of Catholics as a result shifted in emphasis to a worship of the Lord present in the tabernacle or exposed upon the altar rather than an active participation in the celebration of Mass. A varied assortment of Eucharistic practices developed out of this change in attitude.

The Blessed Sacrament was exposed for adoration. People gathered for continuous prayer before the consecrated host, sometimes overnight, sometimes for forty unbroken hours. Fixtures with many candles and incense surrounded these devotions. Processions around the church or community with the exposed sacrament became common. The tabernacle for the reserved sacrament seemed more prominent than, or at least as prominent, as the altar for the sacrifice. People knelt on both knees before the consecrated host.

All of those traditions continued until about the middle of this century when the unofficial and official movements to restore active participation of the people in the Mass began to have substantial impact. As the faithful started to take part more fully in Eucharistic celebrations as sacrifice-banquet memorials of the Lord's Passover event, these devotions to the real presence gradually declined and almost disappeared from many churches. The majority of young people today, for example, probably have never experienced benediction or other such devotional practices.

The Church, in its post-Vatican II rite of *Holy Communion and Worship of the Eucharist Outside Mass*, seeks to put a proper perspective on this aspect of the Eucharist as presence. The following two paragraphs from that document summarizes this teaching:

> The celebration of the eucharist in the sacrifice of the Mass is the true origin and purpose of the worship shown to the eucharist outside Mass. The principal reason for reserving the sacrament after Mass is to unite, through sacramental communion, the faithful unable to participate in the Mass, especially the sick and the aged, with Christ and the offering of his sacrifice.

> In turn, eucharistic reservation, which became customary in order to permit the reception of communion, led to the practice of adoring this sacrament and offering to it the worship which is due to God. This cult of adoration is based upon valid and solid principles. Moreover, some of the public and communal forms of this worship were instituted by the Church itself. [19]

The document then explains in theory and practice how the proper relationship needs to be established between the sacrifice of the Mass, Holy Communion, and adoration of the real presence. Devotion to the reserved sacrament should flow out of and lead to the Eucharistic sacrament, not be in competition with or be separate from the Mass.

Some of the pragmatic steps the document specifies to achieve this integration are:

- The tabernacle should not be on the altar nor the reserved sacrament in the tabernacle from the beginning of Mass. [20]
- The tabernacle should be suitable for private adoration and prayer and ideally in a chapel separate from the body of the church. [21]

- An oil lamp or candle should burn constantly next to the tabernacle as a sign of honor shown to the Lord.[22]
- A single genuflection is made in the presence of the Lord whether reserved in the tabernacle or exposed for public adoration.[23]
- The same number of candles should be used for exposition of the blessed sacrament as for Mass.[24]
- Exposition held exclusively for the giving of benediction is prohibited; the blessing with the Eucharist should be preceded by a suitable period for reading God's word, songs, prayers, and sufficient time for private prayer.[25]

We draw this chapter to a close by quoting from that document on *Holy Communion and Worship of the Eucharist Outside of Mass.* It summarizes the beauty and value of the Eucharist as worship, food, and presence.

> When the faithful honor Christ present in the sacrament, they should remember that this presence is derived from the sacrifice and is directed toward sacramental and spiritual communion.
>
> The same piety which moves the faithful to eucharistic adoration attracts them to a deeper participation in the paschal mystery. It makes them respond gratefully to the gifts of Christ who by his humanity continues to pour divine life upon the members of his body. Living with Christ the Lord, they achieve a close familiarity with him and in his presence pour out their hearts for themselves and for those dear to them; they pray for peace and for the salvation of the world. Offering their entire lives with Christ to the Father in the Holy Spirit, they draw from this wondrous exchange an increase of faith, hope and love. Thus they nourish the proper disposition to celebrate the memorial of the Lord as devoutly as possible and to receive frequently the bread given to us by the Father.
>
> The faithful should make every effort to worship Christ the Lord in the sacrament, depending upon the circumstances of their own life. Pastors should encourage them in this by example and word.[26]

Discussion Questions

1. Give a few examples of things which need to be examined or experienced from various angles for a better if not a full appreciation of their beauty.
2. Where in the New Testament do we find the four accounts describing the institution of the Eucharist at the Last Supper? Look them up and read them through.
3. Is it accurate to say that the Catholic Mass has Jewish roots? If so, in what way would that be true?

4. Why do we celebrate the sabbath on Sunday instead of Saturday as Jewish people and a few other religious bodies do?

5. Could you sketch the general history of the Mass or give its salient elements during the first three centuries? from the Council of Constantine through the Middle Ages? from the Protestant Reformation to the beginning of this century? during modern times?

6. What are the four parts of the Mass according to today's ritual?

7. Many Catholic churches currently offer members the opportunity of receiving Communion under both kinds. Is this a new development or not?

8. Explain the meaning of these three elements expected before a person receives Communion: appropriate knowledge, fasting from food, and freedom from serious sinfulness.

9. Church regulations require that Catholics receive at least once a year and encourage its members to receive frequently, even daily. Why?

10. Do you believe Jesus is truly present under the signs of bread and wine or is there only in a symbolic way? Have you ever participated in a benediction service, a holy hour before the exposed Blessed Sacrament, or a procession with the consecrated host carried in a large vessel called the monstrance? If not, ask your parents, grandparents, an older relative or friend to explain these to you.

PENANCE:

forgiveness
and
growth

5

Penance: Forgiveness and Growth

Just as we better appreciate the richness of the Eucharist by examining that sacrament from different angles, so we will more clearly grasp the beauty of penance by looking at this sacrament from varied perspectives.

Confession

The Sacrament Called Confession.

In *The Rabbi*, a best-selling novel by Noah Gordon, Leslie Rawlings, the daughter of a Congregationalist minister, "confesses" to her friend and date, the young rabbi Michael Kind, an affair she had the previous summer with a Harvard student. He is reluctant to listen to this unburdening of guilt. But the woman insists:

> Yes, don't you see, I haven't been able to tell anybody, but this is so safe. This is practically made to order . . . . It's even better than if I were a Catholic telling it to a priest hidden behind a screen in a confessional, because I *know* the kind of person you are . . . . I apologize . . . I've always wanted to tell somebody about that ever since it happened. I grew so disgusted with myself afterwards . . . .[1]

Prior to the Second Vatican Council, this sacrament of forgiveness and spiritual growth was known to Catholics and to others like Leslie Rawlings almost exclusively by the term "confession."

Churches listed the hours for confession. Priests heard confessions. Repentant sinners made their confessions.

"Confession" clearly communicated the fact that in this sacrament we verbalize our sinfulness, disclose our failures, and mention our mistakes to God's delegate, the priest who then absolves us from the wrong-doing and declares the Lord's forgiveness to us.

Contemporary psychologists have discovered today something that many Catholics knew all along—confessing our sins has enormous value. It can lift burdens, forgive sin, relieve guilt and free people to move on with their lives.

Penance

The Sacrament Called Penance.

Julie came from a long line of atheists who, though Jewish, believed that the world and all the happenings which surround us could be explained in material and scientific ways. However, she had from childhood an almost mystical love for animals and nature. This sense of the sacredness in the universe which she possessed plus other experiences as a child and young adult led her through a gradual conversion process. It reached its culmination when, as a graduate student at the University of California in Berkeley, she felt an inner desire to confess a past wrong-doing to a priest.

She contacted a local pastor and told him of her wish, adding: "I know I cannot receive sacramental absolution. I am not here for psychological counseling. In fact I am not even sure why I came."

He agreed to her request, listened to the tale, spoke briefly of God's mercy, and prayed for her peace. At the end he added an incisive comment about how certain sins which have caused irreparable harm make us realize our human limitations and our deep need for God's forgiveness, guidance, and strength.

That exchange proved to be a turning point in Julie's life, a key which unlocked her heart. Soon thereafter this bright young woman completed the conversion process and became a Catholic. [2]

The word "penance" comes from a Latin and ultimately a Greek term which literally means allowing the spirit to be overturned in order to make it turn towards God. [3] When applied to the sacrament, it accentuates the truth that through this ritual we move through a kind of conversion; we change our hearts under the Lord's grace. Through penance we turn from a state of being separated or distant from God to a state of union or closer union with our Maker; we turn from a condition of darkness and death to one of light and life; we turn from a stance that faces away from Christ to one that faces toward the Lord; we turn from a careless, half-hearted, and lukewarm following of Jesus to a conscientious, single-minded, and fervent pursuit of the Master.

It should be noted that such conversions, like Julie's, are processes and involve time, change, and growth. They are more complex than a simple event or a moment in life. They entail duration, continuity and "not only an event, or a number of isolated events, but a series of related events played out over a period of time."[4]

Reconciliation

The Sacrament Called Reconciliation.

When our ancestors settled in the garden of Eden, they inherited indeed a place of paradise. Friends with God and one another, Adam and Eve found the world of nature at their command and "felt no shame" even though both were naked.

After their fall or sin, all of this changed. They lost their innocence; they hid from God in guilt and were banished by the Lord from the garden; Adam blamed Eve for his misdeed, Eve faulted the serpent and their son Cain killed his brother Abel; plants and animals turned hostile; child-bearing and bread-winning became painful (Gen 2–4).

That familiar story from the Old Testament or Hebrew Scriptures dramatizes the four-fold effect of sin: it ruptures or at least weakens our relationships with God, one another, the world around us, and ourselves. As a consequence, we need a four-fold reconciliation to restore or rebuild those broken or wounded relationships.[5]

When we speak of this sacrament as reconciliation, therefore, our attention turns to the multiple dimensions of sin in terms of relationships and the ability of this ritual to heal the harm caused by our failings.

Each of the terms, confession, penance, and reconciliation, expresses a particular reality about the mystery of this sacrament. Eliminate one aspect and we have an inadequate understanding of the rite; exaggerate one dimension and we develop a distorted concept of the ritual; keep in mind all three approaches and we gain a fuller appreciation of the sacrament. The Church today favors "penance" or "reconciliation," wishing in our time to emphasize the change of heart and elements of relationship rather than the confessing of sin.

Biblical Beginnings

The gentle, merciful, and forgiving nature of Jesus, his ministry and his message will immediately strike any reader of the Gospels.

His very name, given by an angel, means Savior. "You are to name him Jesus because he will save his people from their sins."

His first public task in Galilee was "proclaiming the good news of God" and his initial words, a simple sentence summary of his message, were: "Reform your lives and believe in the gospel" (Matt 1:21; Mark 1:14-15).

His three-year public life included frequent actions whereby he actually forgave sinners: Mary Magdalene, the woman caught in adultery, the paralytic, the thief on the cross.

His teaching and preaching often spoke about forgiveness. We need to ponder only those pivotal parables about the forgiving father and the prodigal son, the lost sheep, and the misplaced coin to grasp that message of mercy.

The Church has traditionally considered the following action and words of Jesus after his resurrection as recorded in John's Gospel to be central in any consideration of the sacrament of penance:

> Then he breathed on them and said:
> "Receive the Holy Spirit.
> If you forgive men's sins,
> they are forgiven them;
> if you hold them bound,
> they are held bound" (John 20:22-23).

While scholars debate in our day whether these were the very words of Christ, whether they prove that Jesus instituted the sacrament as we know it today, and whether those phrases indicate that the Lord bestowed the power to forgive sins only on the apostles, their successors and their chosen delegates, theologians agree that this text of John, in view of other biblical writings, shows that the power to forgive sins was exercised in the early Church.[6]

The history of the exercise of this power to forgive in the Church is harder to uncover and more complex to unravel than even that of the Eucharist. Nevertheless, a few highlights of its development should help us understand better our contemporary practices of penance.

A Brief History

For the first Christians baptism was *the* sacrament for the forgiveness of sins. It symbolized a radical break with sin, darkness, and death and a turning toward God, light, and life. The Church taught then and teaches now that through our baptism we are no longer slaves to sin, but rise with Christ and live for God; through this baptismal washing we receive the forgiveness of sins.[7]

The Church also then and now taught and teaches that in the Eucharist, in the sacrifice of the Mass, the passion of Christ is represented. Jesus' Body given for us and his Blood shed for the forgiveness of sins are offered again by the Church for the salvation of the world. In the Eucharist Christ is present, is offered as the sacrifice which makes our peace with God and brings us together by his Holy Spirit.[8]

The variable Mass prayer texts in modern times illustrate these points. They sometimes speak of our desire that the bread and wine being presented and about to be consecrated forgive our sins. In addition, occasional post Communion prayers plead that the Body and Blood of Christ we have just received may cleanse us from our sins.

The Church once again then and now likewise taught and teaches that the sacrament for the anointing of the sick provides, if necessary, the ill person with the forgiveness of sins.[9]

The Church, finally, then and now taught and teaches that another sacrament, penance, reconciles the faithful who have fallen into sin after baptism. In the words of the fourth-century bishop St. Ambrose, the Church "possesses both waters and tears: the waters of baptism, the tears of penance."[10]

In those initial years baptism occurred generally in adulthood and because of severe opposition from Jewish opponents and secular governments often entailed great hardships. The occasions, therefore, of reconciling persons who had slipped away after baptism seemed fairly infrequent. One necessarily made a major commitment by the very step of becoming a Christian. Lapses, consequently, appeared to be unexpected or isolated.

Eventually, however, the Church had to deal with three major and public failings among some members: apostasy, murder, and adultery. Those who had denied the faith, killed another, or broken the marriage vow and wished to be reconciled during the fourth through the sixth centuries went through a public ceremony of penance. The repentant ones came before the bishop or priest and were

excommunicated liturgically—placed among a group of other penitents and forced to leave Mass at the presentation of the gifts like
the catechumens. After a lengthy period of doing public penance
and proving their repentance, they were reconciled usually on Holy
Thursday through the laying on of hands by the bishop or priest
and allowed to receive Communion. Still, they were required to
do some type of penance for the rest of their lives. Many sinners
in view of that harsh practice understandably put off "conversions"
until near their death beds. [11]

This public penance procedure eventually disappeared and from
the seventh through the eleventh centuries a more private form of
penance, now called confession, developed largely through the influence of Irish monks in Europe. That development included these
practices: Priests as well as bishops ministered penance; minor
offenses were likewise confessed and not merely major or mortal
flaws; penances imposed were less onerous; repentant persons could
receive Communion even before completing their penances; the
priest was less a healer and reconciler and more of a judge; a formula of absolution emerged; the connection between the penitent
and the faith community diminished or even disappeared. [12]

Those trends crystallized during the eleventh through the fourteenth centuries. The idea of making satisfaction or doing penance
for sin was stressed. The actual confession of sins took on a new
dimension and came to be seen as having its own power to reconcile the penitent with God. Contrition or a change of heart likewise received a new focus with the belief that a truly repentant
person was already forgiven before confession. The absolution of
the priest, finally, was judged to be essential, along with confession and contrition. [13]

The Council of Trent in 1551, responding to the objections of
Protestant Reformers about this sacrament, promulgated certain
decrees about penance which have remained standard teaching for
Catholics until the present age: Penance is a sacrament instituted
by Christ separate from baptism; contrition, confession of all serious sins in number and kind, and satisfaction are required of the
penitent; absolution is reserved to the priest alone who must have
jurisdiction or authority to use his power of forgiveness. [14]

The Second Vatican Council ordered that the ritual for penance be revised so it would "more clearly express the nature and
effects of this sacrament." This was accomplished with publication
of the new Rite of Penance in 1973. [15] Pope John Paul II, following
a synod of bishops which discussed the topic, issued an exhortation

on "Reconciliation and Penance" in 1984 containing significant clarifications about some practices and instructions involving the sacrament which have arisen in recent years. [16]

Celebrating Penance Today

The renewed Rite of Penance contains three distinct forms of celebration: a rite for reconciliation of individual penitents; a rite for reconciliation of several penitents with individual confession and absolution; a rite for the reconciliation of several penitents with general confession and absolution.

A mere re-reading of that preceding paragraph exemplifies how this revision flowing from the Second Vatican Council uses almost interchangeably the terms penance, reconciliation, and confession. In what way these reformed rituals seek to foster each dimension of this sacrament should be evident as we examine the structure and content of all three forms.

Rite for Reconciliation of Individual Penitents

Most contemporary Catholics prior to Vatican II experienced the sacrament of penance in private and anonymous fashion, with the encounter normally taking place in a darkened confessional. Some may have received general absolution while serving in the armed forces during war-times and many may have confessed to a priest face-to-face when confined to a hospital bed. But for the vast majority, celebration of this sacrament occurred on a Saturday afternoon or evening kneeling before a screen and whispering memorized formulas and itemized sins to a priest hidden on the other side. A priest pronounced the absolution words in Latin, although around the time of Vatican II permission for and the use of the vernacular for this sacrament became standard in the United States.

Where to Confess

Since the revised ritual encourages the joint reading of Scripture by priest and penitent as well as the laying on of hands-both difficult or impossible in the standard confessional, a different kind of location for this sacrament arose during the seventies. The traditional confession booth, stall or "box" traces its origin only as far back as the period around the Council of Trent in the late sixteenth and early seventeenth century, not a long time as the history of the

Church goes. [17] The United States bishops, empowered by the new ritual to determine the proper place for celebration of this sacrament and seeking to adapt those customary confessionals to the liturgical needs of the reformed rite, decreed in 1974:

> It is considered desirable that small chapels or rooms of reconciliation be provided in which penitents might choose to confess their sins through an informal face-to-face exchange with the priest, with the opportunity for appropriate spiritual counsel. It would also be regarded as desirable that such chapels or rooms be designed to afford the option of the penitent's kneeling at the fixed confessional grill in the usual way, but in every case the freedom of the penitent is to be respected.

A few years later the Bishops' Committee on the Liturgy for this country expanded on that decision, suggesting in a 1978 document on *Environment and Art in Catholic Worship:*

> A room or rooms for the reconciliation of individual penitents may be located near the baptismal area (when it is at the entrance) or in another convenient place. Furnishings and decoration should be simple and austere, offering the penitent a choice between face-to-face encounter or the anonymity provided by a screen, with nothing superfluous in evidence beyond a simple cross, table and Bible. The purpose of this room is primarily for the celebration of the reconciliation liturgy; it is not a lounge, counseling room, etc. The word "chapel" more appropriately describes this space. [18]

Requests for information about reconciliation rooms in an informal survey of this country in 1983 revealed that about 75 percent of the United States parishes now have some form of a reconciliation chapel which provides the option of anonymous or face-to-face confessions.

How to Confess

This renewed first form for reconciliation does not differ radically from the customary procedures of pre-Vatican II years. There remains a confession of sins, exchange with the priest, act of contrition, words of absolution, and an assigned work of satisfaction. However, it offers a variety of prayers, biblical texts, and expressions of repentance for the celebration, together with the possibility for the laying on of hands during the pronouncement of the forgiveness formula. The structure proposed and these rich available resources seek to inject a freshness of approach for each experience of the sacrament and an elimination or diminution of routine confessions.

Here is an outline of the rite for reconciliation of individual penitents:

1. RECEPTION OF THE PENITENT

After the priest warmly welcomes and kindly greets the penitent, both together make the Sign of the Cross.

The priest then prays for the penitent who, at the end, answers: Amen.

2. READING OF THE WORD OF GOD

The priest either from memory or by reading may, if the situation is suitable, recite a passage of Scripture which speaks about God's mercy or calls us to conversion and a change of heart.

3. CONFESSION OF SINS AND ACCEPTANCE OF SATISFACTION

The penitent confesses his or her sins; the priest, after discussing with the penitent his or her spiritual state and giving appropriate counsel, assigns an act of penance or satisfaction.

4. PRAYER OF PENITENT AND ABSOLUTION

The penitent expresses sorrow for sin by reciting the traditional formula, one of the ten new prayers given, or similar personal words of contrition.

The priest then extends his hands over the penitent's head (or at least extends his right hand) and pronounces the formula of absolution.

The penitent listens prayerfully and, at the conclusion, responds: Amen.

5. PROCLAMATION OF PRAISE OF GOD AND DISMISSAL

The priest says:
"Give thanks to the Lord, for he is good."
The penitent concludes:
"His mercy endures forever."

The priest then dismisses the penitent with a prayer or suitable phrase and the penitent responds: "Amen" or "Thank you."[19]

Why Confess

Some question today the reason behind this sacrament. Why, the issue may be stated, confess to a priest? Why not to a friend, an advisor, or a community of people? Why not directly to God alone?

As we have seen, the Church upholds the teaching that perfect sorrow or contrition can bring God's forgiveness and grace without confession to a priest. At the same time, Church law requires that serious sins ordinarily be confessed prior to Communion. Apart from this legislation, why should a person confess to a priest?

Here are a few reasons in support of the practice:

- The priest freely ministers this sacrament of reconciliation. He freely received from God the power to declare sins forgiven in Jesus' name and thus must freely exercise for others that ministry of mercy.
- The priest strictly keeps confidences learned in confession. Church laws governing what we term the seal of confession prohibit under severest penalty a priest from revealing any sin of an individual penitent to any person under any conditions. The long history of this sacrament indicates that priests, despite their sometimes human weaknesses in other areas, have nevertheless observed those restrictions remarkably well. Confessors take these rules very, very seriously.
- The priest's wide experience acquired through regularly hearing many confessions gives him wide insights into human guilt and divine mercy.
- The priest pronounces with authority and in an audible voice God's forgiveness of sins. "Through the ministry of the Church may God give you pardon and peace, and I absolve you from your sins in the name of the Father, and of the Son, and of the Holy Spirit." The person who confesses walks away having actually heard these clear and certain words of liberation. She or he knows the guilt is gone and the sins removed. Friends, advisors, and others can comfort or reassure on this matter, but not announce with such certitude.
- The priest carries out the promises of Christ given to the apostles and his followers that they would have the power to forgive sins.
- The priest seeks to mirror in his attitude, words, and actions the gentleness of Christ. There are over a dozen incidents in the Gospels which either describe Jesus actually forgiving the repentant sinner or teaching about the mercy of God which has no limit and lasts forever. Priests set the Savior's example as their role model in hearing confessions.
- The priest and the penitent actually celebrate a sacrament, the sacrament of penance or reconciliation. Confession of sins with absolution is more than a merely human ritual cleansing away unpleasant guilt. As one of the seven sacraments established by Christ, penance not only forgives sins, but also restores or increases sanctifying grace. Moreover, reconciliation bestows actual graces which heal wounds caused by our sins and strengthen virtues needed for our progress.
- The priest in the name of the Church reconciles us with the community. Sin, as we have seen, weakens or ruptures our relationships with God, others and the world around us. In this sacrament, the priest both declares those fractured relationships have been restored and aids in rebuilding them. [20]

Rite for Reconciliation of Several Penitents with Individual Confession and Absolution

Within the past decade most American parishes during Advent and Lent began to host communal penance services. Advertised in advance and with neighboring clergy usually invited to assist, the celebrations generally attract sizeable crowds.

The services more or less observe the format provided by the ritual, although there are significant variations. After an opening song, greeting, and prayer, there follows several appropriate scriptural readings, a homily, an examination of conscience, and joint recitation of expressions of sorrow. The assembled priests then disperse to different locations for the hearing of individual confessions.

The ritual suggests, when all have completed their confessions, that the community reassemble and sing a song of praise. The celebration concludes with a prayer and dismissal blessing. [21]

Because there often are extensive delays before the confessions finish and many participants simply leave, it is increasingly standard practice to drop the concluding song, prayer, and dismissal, making the rite "open-ended." The clergy thus continue until all have been heard and may be engaged with the work of reconciling individual penitents for an hour or more following the beginning word service.

Such penance celebrations obviously provide participants with a more substantial proclamation of God's Word about sin and forgiveness than is feasible in the first form of reconciliation. In addition, this rite emphasizes the four-fold and common dimension of sin and reconciliation described at the start of this chapter. In the words of the ritual's introduction:

> Communal celebration shows more clearly the ecclesial nature of penance. The faithful listen together to the word of God, which proclaims his mercy and invites them to conversion; at the same time they examine the conformity of their lives with that word of God and help each other through common prayer. After each person has confessed his sins and received absolution, all praise God together for his wonderful deeds on behalf of the people he has gained for himself through the blood of his Son. [22]

Through common prayer, common song, common hearing of God's Word, common examination of conscience, common expression of sorrow, and common presence together, participants should better understand that sin ruptures or weakens our relationship not only with God but also with others. Hence reconciliation needs to be with the Lord and with others.

Rite for Reconciliation of Several Penitents with General Confession and Reconciliation

During war times in the past Catholic chaplains prior to an approaching battle would impart general absolution to the assembled troops. Since he normally was the only priest available, since there were countless Catholic soldiers before him and since the conflict was imminent, the priest could according to Church law give absolution to all without individual confession of sins by each penitent. Those with grave or serious sins were told, however, that while these faults had been forgiven, they had the responsibility of confessing them in an individual manner at the first opportunity.

The revised ritual provides a better liturgical celebration for such general absolution situations than was available in the past. The conditions for its use, however, remain essentially the same. As noted in the ritual's introduction, they are:

- Individual, integral confession and absolution remain the only ordinary way for the faithful to reconcile themselves with God and the Church, unless physical or moral impossibility excuses from this kind of confession.
- Particular, occasional circumstances may render it lawful and even necessary to give general absolution to a number of penitents without their previous individual confession.
- In addition to cases involving danger of death, as in the war-time situation noted above, the Church approves giving sacramental absolution on other occasions to a number of people at the same time after they have made only a generic confession. The penitents, of course, must be suitably called to repentance and be contrite of heart. There also must exist a grave need. This serious spiritual necessity may arise when, in view of the large number of penitents, there are not a sufficient amount of confessors available to hear individual confessions properly and within a suitable period of time. Because of that circumstance the penitents would, through no fault of their own, be forced to go without sacramental grace for a long period.
- Such a possibility clearly occurs often in mission territories where a single priest may have responsibility for thousands of Catholics in a widespread area. He physically could not hear each person's confession and grant individual absolution. That situation, however, also may develop in countries like the United States when, particularly during Advent or Lent, a huge, unexpected crowd of

penitents appear for a common penance service or scheduled period of reconciliation. In those cases, too, the one or few priest confessors present could not properly and within a suitable period of time hear each confession.

- Those who receive pardon for grave sins by a common absolution should go to individual confession before they receive this kind of absolution again, unless they are impeded by a just reason. They are strictly bound, unless this is morally impossible, to go to confession within a year. The precept which obliges each of the faithful to confess at least once a year to a priest all the grave sins which that person has not individually confessed before also remains in force in this case too.[23]

One United States bishop of a mission-like territory, soon after the revised ritual appeared, authorized priests of his diocese to grant general absolution during Lent. Many of his parishes were scattered, often separated by considerable distance and accessible only by difficult water or expensive air travel. Because of a parish's small size and isolated nature, the members seldom if ever saw or had recourse to any priest other than their pastor who, furthermore, knew them only too well. Such a combination of circumstances made confession to him a physical possibility, but a moral impossibility. They could, in that case, conceivably be excused from confessing individually to him after general absolution and even receive general absolution again without that individualized confession.

At the 1983 Synod of Bishops in Rome, several bishops, notably from mission countries, urged a more extensive use of general absolution and the elimination of the requirement to confess grave sins later in an individual way.[24] Pope John Paul II, nevertheless, in his exhortation of 1984 following the Synod, repeated the traditional regulations:

> While it is true that, when the conditions required by canonical discipline occur, use may be made of the third form of celebration, it must not be forgotten that this form cannot become an ordinary one, and it cannot and must not be used—as the Synod repeated—except "in cases of grave necessity." And there remains unchanged the obligation to make an individual confession of serious sins before again having recourse to another general absolution.[25]

A Sacrament of Forgiveness and Growth

The Church from its earliest years to modern days has celebrated the sacrament of penance in a wide variety of ways. But the purpose has always been the same: to make present for repentant believers the good news of God's forgiveness.

For those heavily burdened with guilt, cut off from the Lord, and deprived of full membership in the Church or the Eucharist, this sacrament can be a magnificent source of joy and peace. In it Christ forgives the sin, dissolves the guilt, embraces the sinner, and restores the alienated to communion at God's table.

As a married woman and mother remarked: "After returning to confession for the first time in twelve years, I feel so clean, so whole, and so loved that I can only ask: Why did I wait so long, endure so much sorrow and suffering when the Lord was there all the time?"[26]

For those not so heavily burdened and who judge that, despite minor faults and failings, they are walking with the Lord, this sacrament often seems less attractive than it once did. At least, these people approach penance or reconciliation less frequently even though they participate in the Eucharist regularly and consider themselves as good members of the Church.

Conscious that only confession of grave or mortal sins is required by Church law, those who formerly received this sacrament every few weeks or months may today seek out penance perhaps only on a yearly basis or even less often. The Church expresses disappointment at this trend because it means that the unique opportunities which reconciliation offers for spiritual growth are lost.

Pope John Paul II, for example, noted:

> Great importance must continue to be given to teaching the faithful also to make use of the Sacrament of Penance for venial sins alone, as is borne out by a centuries-old doctrinal tradition and practice.
>
> Though the Church knows and teaches that venial sins are forgiven in other ways too—for instance, by acts of sorrow, works of charity, prayer, penitential rites—she does not cease to remind everyone of the special usefulness of the sacramental moment for these sins too. The frequent use of the sacrament—to which some categories of the faithful are in fact held—strengthens the awareness that even minor sins offend God and harm the Church, the Body of Christ. Its celebration then becomes for the faithful "the occasion and the incentive to conform themselves more closely to Christ and to make themselves more docile to the voice of the Spirit." Above all it should be emphasized that the grace proper to the sacramental celebration has a great remedial power and helps to remove the very roots of sin.[27]

The person burdened with serious sin need but believe in Jesus' mercy and have the courage to approach this sacrament of forgiveness. The location, the words and the format, for example, are relatively insignificant elements. A mere opening of the heart will, as it did for Julie, allow God's peace-giving love to rush in and dispel the gloom or guilt.

The person not conscious of any serious fault, but perhaps a bit complacent or too comfortable with her or his Christianity may have to work harder to discover or rediscover the power of this ritual as a sacrament of growth.[28] Such people may need to develop a renewed attitude which understands that "frequent and careful celebration of this sacrament is also very useful as a remedy for venial sins . . . . is a serious striving to perfect the grace of baptism so that, as we bear in our body the death of Jesus Christ, his life may be seen in us even more clearly."[29]

Discussion Questions

1. Recall a time when after some wrongdoing you felt a need to confess and told a parent, a close friend, or a priest in confession about the misdeed. Do you remember your reaction afterwards?

2. Can you identify an occasion in your life during which you wanted to change directions, like stop smoking, or decide about your future, like selecting a career, job or college? Was the step or decision instantaneous or did it involve a rather long and somewhat difficult process?

3. Sin breaks or wounds our relationships with God, others, the world around us, and our inner selves. Try to think of examples affecting each of the four ruptured or weakened relationships, for example, a carelessly dropped match causing a fire which destroyed acres of precious timber or an alcoholic parent bringing great hurt to spouse and children.

4. Could you cite a few incidents in which Jesus forgave a sinner or spoke about forgiveness? If not, glance through the Gospels and note five illustrations of Christ the merciful one either forgiving or speaking about forgiveness.

5. Is confession or the sacrament of penance the only way the Church forgives sins? Explain.

6. Does your parish church or churches in your area have reconciliation rooms or chapels? Have you confessed both "face-to-face" and anonymously or behind a partition? Which manner do you prefer and why?

7. Could you give an interested inquirer several cogent reasons why Catholics confess to a priest?
8. Have you ever participated in a communal penance service with individual confession and absolution? What were your reactions? Why does the Church recommend these?
9. What are three situations in which general absolution without individual confession of sin has been used by priests in the relatively recent past?
10. Explain the meaning of penance or reconciliation as a sacrament of forgiveness and growth.

ANOINTING:

healing,
courage,
and
hope

6

Anointing: Healing, Courage, and Hope

Anyone with a sympathetic face, an understanding heart, and a good ear soon learns how many people hurt in this world. In fact, every person who reads these lines has her or his own story of past or present pain.

The pain may obviously be physical, from a childhood case of chicken pox, which for a few days caused 125 sores on the youngster's back, to a crippling arthritic condition, which for countless years has made each morning, each day, and each move a struggle for the afflicted individual.

The pain may be mental or emotional, less evident to others, perhaps, but possibly even more distressing than physical aches to the suffering person. Those inner pains might range from a teenager's worry about acceptance to one spouse's feeling of rejection by the other to an executive's deep depression over unemployment to a senior citizen's fear about tomorrow and tomorrow and tomorrow.

It has always been thus. Since the time after Adam and Eve's bad decisions in the Garden, life has not been a paradise, but rather a mix of pleasure and pain, of hurts and, sometimes, healings.

Jesus, the Master Healer

Jesus entered into such a world. Like us, he hurt at times, experiencing himself the emotional and mental anguish of another garden, Gethsemani, and the physical pain of the cross at Calvary. Christ also, as we do, encountered countless people with afflictions of every kind.

But there was a difference. The Lord possessed both the desire and the power to ease those pains, heal those wounds, and lift those spirits. This excerpt from Matthew's Gospel succinctly describes Christ as the Master Healer:

> Jesus toured all of Galilee. He taught in their synagogues, proclaimed the good news of the kingdom, and cured the people of every disease and illness. As a consequence of this, his reputation traveled the length of Syria. They carried to him all those afflicted with various diseases and racked with pain: the possessed, the lunatics, the paralyzed. He cured them all (Matt 4:23-24).

It is fascinating to note that nearly one fifth of the Gospel texts is given over to Christ's healings and to discussions prompted by these cures. Thus, of the 3,779 verses in the Gospels, 727 specifically treat physical or mental healings and instances of resurrection from the dead. Moreover, 165 verses speak about eternal life, and 31 incidents or references touch upon miracles which include healing.

There are 41 distinct physical and mental healings (72 if you count duplications) recounted in the Gospels plus the innumerable cures covered by general references to a healing of crowds, or multitudes. [1]

Sharing His Power

Magnificent as were the deeds of this miracle working Messiah, even more marvelous is the fact that he entrusted his power of healing to others.

First to the Twelve: He "gave them authority to expel unclean spirits and to cure sickness and disease of every kind" (Matt 10:1).

Next to the seventy-two disciples: "Into whatever city you go, after they welcome you, eat what they set before you, and cure the sick there" (Luke 10:8-9).

Finally, to all believers: "Signs like these will accompany those who have professed their faith: they will use my name to expel demons . . . and the sick upon whom they lay their hands will recover" (Mark 16:17-18).

The following incident involving Jesus, the way he shared his power to heal and the manner in which that delegation was carried out has particular significance for us in this examination of the sacrament for the anointing of the sick. Mark's Gospel tells us: "Jesus summoned the Twelve and began to send them out two by two, giving them authority over unclean spirits . . . . With that they went off preaching the need of repentance. They expelled many demons, anointed the sick with oil, and worked many cures" (Mark 6:7, 12-13).

It should not surprise us that they anointed the sick with oil, since during those days this was a common procedure. At the time of Jesus and even before that, people used oil, (especially olive oil) for many purposes—some merely practical and others quite religious. Among its many uses, oil was employed for cooking and eating, for the light of lamps, for a cleansing substance in bathing similar to soap today, for cosmetics and healing medicines, for protection against the dry climate, for a symbol of joy, for a sign of respect, and for preparation of the dead.

Jewish tradition, perhaps absorbing a custom from the surrounding Egyptian and Canaanite cultures, also developed the practice of anointing persons and objects with oil, thereby setting them aside for religious or sacred use. Thus, to illustrate, the Hebrew Scriptures tell us priests, prophets, and kings were anointed and by that action consecrated to God's service.[2]

The Sacrament of Anointing the Sick

When Pope Paul VI introduced the revised ritual for this sacrament after the Second Vatican Council, he cited that above incident from Mark with its reference to anointing the sick with oil as an "intimation" of the sacrament and its institution by Christ. In doing so he was repeating the teachings of the Council of Trent which stated further that the sacrament was "recommended to the faithful and made known" by James the apostle and brother of the Lord.[3]

The following excerpt from the Epistle of James is the classic biblical passage employed to establish and explain the sacrament of anointing of the sick and is also used frequently within celebrations of the rite itself:

> If anyone among you is suffering hardship, he must pray. If a person is in good spirits, he should sing a hymn of praise. Is there anyone sick among you? He should ask for the presbyters of the Church. They in turn are to pray over him, anointing him with oil in the Name [of the Lord]. This prayer uttered in faith will reclaim the one who is ill, and the Lord will restore him to health. If he has

committed any sins, forgiveness will be his. Hence, declare your sins to one another, and pray for one another, that you may find healing (5:13-16).

History of the Sacrament

The action described or recommended by James clearly foreshadowed what was to become the practice of the Church over ensuing centuries and is our own today. As might be expected, however, the history of anointing in the Church, while continuous, nevertheless remains vague, particularly during early years, and has experienced several shifts in emphasis over the centuries.

In general, we see at the beginning a concentration upon the sacrament as one intended primarily for healing the sick; then the main thrust came to consider this as a rite or sacrament for the dying; finally, in recent centuries and our own day, there has been a gradual return to considering the sacrament of anointing with oil as primarily concerned about healing the hurting. The preparation-for-dying aspect has been taken up by viaticum or Communion ministered under a special formula for a person critically ill.

For the first eight-hundred years, there is every indication from the writings of Church Fathers, liturgical documents, and lives of the saints that the Church anointed those who were sick. However, we are not absolutely clear about the way this was done, other than to note these salient elements: (1) The oil, presented by the faithful, was blessed by the bishop. That blessing, viewed as the most important part of the rite, gave the oil a divine power and placed it in the category of a sacrament. (2) The application of the oil was entrusted not only to the presbyters but likewise to lay persons who would anoint themselves, sick relatives, and ill friends. (3) A prayer of some sort normally accompanied the anointing as did usually the laying on of hands. (4) People applied the oil externally but also might at times take it internally by consuming it. (5) The anointing was not seen as a preparation for death but as a ritual to restore bodily and spiritual health.

From the ninth century until the Council of Trent in the sixteenth century, a radical shift occurred in the use of this anointing rite. It became a sacrament for the dying instead of a ritual to restore health. More specifically: (1) The anointing itself was restricted to presbyters or priests. (2) A more formal ritual evolved with precise prayers to be recited. (3) Priests began to anoint the five senses—eyes, ears, nose, mouth, hands—and to join each anointing with a prayer which linked it with the forgiveness of sins; for example, "May the Lord forgive you by this holy anointing and his most loving mercy, whatever sins you have committed by the use of your sight, etc. Amen." (4) The anointing was connected with deathbed conversions and began to be viewed as a sacrament for the dying. (5) The sacrament came to be called "Extreme Unction," or the last anointing, since it was the final anointing to be received in this life and before death. (6) The order for the sick shifted from penance, anointing, and viaticum to penance, viaticum, and anointing. (7) The principal effect sought was no longer the restoration of health but a preparation for the glory of heaven after death. (8) Extreme Unction, also unhappily becoming known as "the last rites," was seen to remove our sins and the remnants of our sins, strengthen us in the final battle, and speed our passage to God after death.

The period from the Council of Trent until the Second Vatican Council saw a gradual but not complete return to the practice of James and the early Church: (1) The Council of Trent providentially did not continue the restrictions of the earlier period. On the contrary, it said that the sacrament was to be given "especially"—instead of "only"—to those who are so dangerously ill that they seem close to death. (2) It confirmed that priests were the proper ministers of the sacrament. (3) It upheld the teaching that this was a true sacrament, one of the seven, and traced its origin to Christ through Mark and James. (4) It listed, without priority, the triple effects of this sacrament: to take away sin and its remains; to strengthen the sick person inwardly or spiritually during the struggle of sickness and dying; to restore bodily health when that will prove beneficial for the welfare of the entire person. This particular teaching most significantly opened up the possibility of returning to the original practice within the Church. (5) During the centuries following Trent, Church practice became more and more lenient in its interpretation of what "danger of death" meant and also stressed the health-restoring power of the sacrament. (6) Popes during the twentieth century frequently urged those who care for the seriously sick and dying to summon the priest early for this sacrament so that its beneficial effects might be received by the ill individual. (7) Nevertheless, the concept of "last rites" persisted and Catholics in general continued to fear the sacrament. Family, friends, or medical personnel would only with reluctance summon the clergy.

Such a call seemed to indicate that all hope had gone and certain death lay ahead.

That slow reversal, however, set the stage for the treatment of this sacrament by the bishops gathered at Rome during the 1960s for the Second Vatican Council. In the Constitution on the Sacred Liturgy (paragraphs 72–75), they decreed the following:

> (1) Extreme Unction more fittingly should be called "Anointing of the Sick." (2) It is not a sacrament only for those at the point of death. (3) As soon as anyone begins to be in danger of death from sickness or old age, it is fitting to anoint the person. (4) The continuous order for the seriously ill is restored to penance, anointing, and viaticum. (5) The number of anointings and the prayers were to be revised to correspond better to today's varying needs. [4]

The Sacrament Today

Soon after Pope Paul VI issued the official Latin text for the revised rite for the anointing and pastoral care of the sick in 1972, the American bishops, among others, approved a provisional English translation of the document and published a new ritual for use by priests of the United States in serving those who are ill.

After a decade of experience with that book, the conference of bishops in this country produced a finalized version containing considerable adaptations suggested by those who had employed the initial volume. The 1982 publication *Pastoral Care of the Sick: Rites of Anointing and Viaticum* reflects the Church's current approach to this matter not only by its actual content but also through its title and format.

Pastoral Care of the Sick thus contains two distinct liturgical elements: a rite of anointing and a rite for viaticum. Part I ("Pastoral Care of the Sick") includes visitation, Communion, and anointing of the sick. Part II ("Pastoral Care of the Dying") contains the ritual for viaticum, commendation of the dying, and prayers for the dead.

By that division, the Church clearly teaches that anointing today is more a sacrament of healing and support for the sick rather than a ritual for the dying. Moreover, it indicates that viaticum—Communion with a special format and formula—is the Church's official rite for those in danger of or near death. [5]

Healing and Courage

Part I of this text, "Pastoral Care of the Sick" includes, as mentioned, the rite of anointing together with visitation and Communion for the sick. The ceremonies, readings and prayers in that portion of the ritual have as their purpose "to comfort the sick in time of anxiety, to encourage them to fight against illness, and perhaps restore them to health."[6]

The sacrament of anointing of the sick itself provides those who are seriously ill with possibly a restoration of health and certainly the special help of God's grace in their time of anxiety "lest they be broken in spirit, and under the pressure of temptation, perhaps weakened in their faith."[7]

The list of its effects below, taken from the Vatican II restored ritual, will show how the Church has returned almost precisely to the position on anointing described in James 5:14-16. As an overall result, the Church declares that this sacrament "gives the grace of the Holy Spirit to those who are sick." More specifically that means: (1) "By this grace the whole person is helped and saved, sustained by trust in God, and strengthened against the temptations of the Evil One and against anxiety over death. Thus the sick person is able not only to bear suffering bravely but also to fight against it." (2) "A return to health may follow the reception of this sacrament if it will be beneficial to the sick person's salvation." (3) "If necessary, the sacrament also provides the sick person with the forgiveness of sins and the completion of Christian penance."[8]

The readings, prayers, blessings, and gestures of the ritual naturally reflect their teaching about the effects of the sacrament. Thus:

"The grace of the Holy Spirit to those who are sick": The formula which accompanies the actual anointing with oil reads in part, "Through this holy anointing may the Lord in his love and mercy help you with the grace of the Holy Spirit."[9]

"To bear suffering bravely": A prayer recited over the person(s) to be anointed conveys that notion, asking for God's help for the sick so that they might indeed bear their burdens bravely. Another petition, also to be used after the anointing, contains similar thoughts: "Support him/her with your power, comfort him/her with your protection, and give him/her the strength to fight against evil. Since you have given him/her a share in your own passion, help him/her to find hope in suffering."[10]

"A return to health": The blessings at the end of the ceremony include these requests: "May God the Son heal you . . . . May God restore you to health and grant you salvation.[11]

"The forgiveness of sins": A general prayer after the anointing explicitly mentions this effect. "Heal his/her sickness and forgive his/her sins; expel all afflictions of mind and body . . . ."[12]

Who Is to Be Anointed

The general principle determining who may be appropriately anointed is this: "Great care should be taken to see that those of the faithful whose health is seriously impaired by sickness or old age receive this sacrament."

The phrase "seriously impaired" is the key element in this norm. The sick person need not be gravely, dangerously, or perilously ailing to be eligible for the sacrament. On the other hand, people slightly ill—for example, with a minor cold or headache—are not proper candidates for anointing.

The ritual, nevertheless, wishes the words "seriously impaired" to be interpreted liberally and without anxiety. "A prudent and reasonably sure judgment, without scruple, is sufficient for deciding on the seriousness of an illness; if necessary a doctor may be consulted." [13]

Here are some practical applications of the general norm to common situations: (1) The sacrament may be repeated if the sick person recovers after being anointed and then again falls ill or if during the same illness the person's condition becomes more serious. (2) In the case of a person who is chronically ill, or elderly and in a weakened condition, the sacrament of anointing may be repeated when in the pastoral judgment of the priest the condition of the sick person warrants the repetition of the sacrament. (3) A sick person may be anointed before surgery whenever a serious illness is the reason for the surgery. (4) Elderly people may be anointed if they have become notably weakened even though no serious illness is present. (5) Sick children may be anointed if they have sufficient use of reason to be stengthened by this sacrament. (6) The sacrament of anointing may be conferred upon sick people who, although they have lost consciousness or the use of reason, would, as Christian believers, probably have asked for it were they in control of their faculties. (7) When a priest has been called to attend those who are already dead, he should not administer the sacrament of anointing. Instead, he should pray for them, asking that God forgive their sins and graciously receive them into the kingdom. But if the priest is doubtful whether the sick person is dead, he may give the sacrament conditionally. (8) Some types of mental sickness are now classified as serious. Those who are judged to have a serious mental illness and who would be strengthened by the sacrament may be anointed. The anointing may be repeated in accordance with the conditions for other kinds of serious illness.

The Church very strongly urges that relatives, friends, or health-care personnel summon the priest early on in a serious illness so that the sick individual may receive the sacrament "with full faith and devotion."[14]

The Actual Anointing

Pope Paul VI decreed that the essential sacramental rite consists of anointing the seriously ill on the forehead and hands with blessed olive oil or another blessed plant oil while saying these words:

(While anointing the forehead) "Through this holy anointing may the Lord in his love and mercy help you with the grace of the Holy Spirit."

(While anointing the hands) "May the Lord who frees you from sin save you and raise you up."

In case of necessity, however, the priest may give a single anointing on the forehead or, because of the sick person's particular condition, on another suitable part of the body (such as the general area of pain or injury).[15]

Earlier we observed how both Mark and James mentioned the use of oil as a means and a sign of healing. The new ritual continues this practice of anointing the sick with oil to signify healing, strengthening, and the presence of the Spirit. It has a further connotation of soothing and comforting the sick and of restoring the tired and the weak. Since illness can physically and spiritually debilitate the sick person, this oil strengthens the person to fight off these detrimental effects in his or her struggle.

Laying on of Hands

Jesus often healed people by laying his hands upon them or through a simple gesture of touching them. The Church in its revised ritual restores this gesture immediately before the prayer over the oil and the anointing itself.

The rubric, or directive, reads: "In silence, the priest lays his hands on the head of the sick person."[16]

A litany precedes that gesture and may include this phrase: "Give life and health to our brother/sister N., on whom we lay our hands in your name."[17]

The laying on of hands signifies that: (1) The Church is praying for the Holy Spirit to come upon the sick person. (2) The Church blesses the person as we pray for the power of God's healing grace to restore the sick individual to health or at least to strengthen him or her in time of illness. (3) The entire Church throughout the world is in solidarity with and praying for the sick person. (4) The Church is doing what Jesus did, touching or laying hands upon the ill one. (5) The Church is bringing forgiveness and reconciliation. (6) The Church wishes to be present and close to the seriously ill person who often feels isolated, alone, and abandoned or rejected.[18]

Faith

Jesus did on occasion heal persons without faith, but usually belief was a condition for the cure or a reason behind it. Moreover, his wondrous deeds had as their ultimate goal to bring people to faith in him and his message.

The Church, with its reformed ritual, wishes to resurrect that approach and to stress the importance of faith for the effective celebration of this sacrament. Thus, "In the anointing of the sick, which includes the prayer of faith (see James 5:15), faith itself is manifested. Above all, this faith must be made actual both in the minister of the sacrament and, even more importantly, in the recipient. The sick person will be saved by personal faith and the faith of the Church, which looks back to the death and resurrection of Christ, the source of the sacrament's power (see Jas 5:15), and looks ahead to the future kingdom that is pledged in the sacraments."[19]

There are several pragmatic ways in which this faith dimension can be more fully developed during the anointing ritual.

Providing there is time, the priest would first seek to become acquainted with the patient and the family, as well as speak with others involved (including the health-care personnel).

In the course of his first and subsequent visits, he would talk about the sacrament, its purpose, and the bond which exists among all members of the Church. He would emphasize that through our common faith and common baptism we are members of the Body of Christ. Because of that link the sufferings of one are the sufferings of all. Our prayer and this sacrament, he would continue, is done in the name and power of Jesus and his entire Church. Thus their own faith, joined with the faith of the whole body of believers, is powerful indeed. Such words would bring support and hope for both the ill individual and all who care for him or her.

He might then describe the various readings and prayers available as options for them in the anointing ceremony and set a specific time for all to be on hand.

During the actual celebration of the rite, they would as a result, join in the prayers, hear God's Word, perhaps hold or touch the sick one, and possibly sing appropriate songs. Their faith and the faith of the seriously ill patient would be expressed and deepened.

The faith dimension is also enhanced when the parish community prays for the sick person at Sunday Mass.

Communal celebrations with several to be anointed, a number of priests concelebrating, and an assembly of supporters present, now provided and encouraged by the ritual, likewise enhances the faith dimension of the sacrament.

Food for the Sick

The Church wishes to offer the Eucharist, Holy Communion, for those who are ill and confined to their homes or to health care institutions. Introductory guidelines of the ritual urge pastoral leaders to provide frequent, even daily, opportunities for Communion for the sick or confined. "Priests with pastoral responsibilities should see to it that the sick or aged, even though not seriously ill or in danger of death are given every opportunity to receive the eucharist frequently, even daily, especially during the Easter season."[20]

These directives recognize that priests or pastoral staff people probably cannot handle this obligation alone. They move on, therefore, to support the appointment of additional extraordinary ministers of the Eucharist. "To provide frequent communion for the sick, it may be necessary to ensure that the community has a sufficient number of ministers of communion."[21]

The norms also encourage connecting the Sunday Eucharist with the community's concern and care for the sick:

> The links between the community's eucharistic celebration, espe cially on the Lord's Day, and the communion of the sick are inti mate and manifold. Besides remembering the sick in the genera. intercessions at Mass, those present should be reminded occasionally of the significance of communion in the lives of those who are ill: union with Christ in his struggle with evil, his prayer for the world, and his love for the Father, and union with the community from which they are separated.
>
> The obligation to visit and comfort those who cannot take part in the eucharistic assembly may be clearly demonstrated by taking communion to them from the community's eucharistic celebration. This symbol of unity between the community and its sick members has the deepest significance on the Lord's Day, the special day of the eucharistic assembly.[22]

A rapidly growing number of parishes in the United States are implementing these recommendations. They have trained a corps of special ministers of mercy to the sick who participate at Sunday Eucharist, then take the Lord's Body to one or a few persons restricted to their homes, apartments, or rooms. There they read the scriptural texts for the day's Mass, summarize the homily, read the ritual prayers, minister Communion, and after a friendly visit leave a copy of the parish bulletin.

While these arrangements are more or less ongoing, one detects and should expect the gradual expansion of this practice on a more informal temporary basis—that is, spouse bringing Holy Communion home to one's spouse, parent to children, children to parents, or relative to relative throughout a temporary or short-term illness.

Hope for the Dying

Viaticum is more truly today the Church's liturgical rite for those who are dying. The word means, literally, "(food) with you on the way." In the introduction to this ritual the text states:

> The celebration of the eucharist as viaticum, food for the passage through death to eternal life, is the sacrament proper to the dying Christian. It is the completion and crown of the Christian life on this earth, signifying that the Christian follows the Lord to eternal glory and the banquet of the heavenly kingdom.[23]

Here are several practical points stressed by the ritual in connection with viaticum:

The purpose of viaticum and the other rites in Part II of the ritual book is "to comfort and strengthen a dying Christian in the passage from this life. The ministry to the dying places emphasis on trust in the Lord's promise of eternal life rather than on the struggle against illness which is characteristic of the pastoral care of the sick.[24]

The entire Christian community, not simply the clergy or the family, has a duty to care for the dying person. "The Christian community has a continuing responsibility to pray for and with the person who is dying. Through its sacramental ministry to the dying the community helps Christians to embrace death in mysterious union with the crucified and risen Lord, who awaits them in the fullness of life."[25]

"Whenever it is possible, the dying Christian should be able to receive viaticum within Mass. In this way he or she shares fully, during the final moments of this life, in the eucharistic sacrifice, which proclaims the Lord's own passing through death to life. However, circumstances, such as confinement to a hospital ward or the very emergency which makes death imminent, may frequently make the complete eucharistic celebration impossible. In this case, the rite for viaticum outside Mass is appropriate."[26]

"A distinctive feature of the celebration of viaticum, whether within or outside Mass is the renewal of the baptismal profession of faith by the dying person. This occurs after the homily and replaces the usual form of the profession of faith. Through the baptismal profession at the end of earthly life, the one who is dying uses the language of his or her initial commitment, which is renewed each Easter and on other occasions in the Christian life. In the context of viaticum, it is a renewal and fulfillment of initiation into the Christian mysteries, baptism leading to the eucharist."[27]

"The rites for viaticum within and outside Mass may include the sign of peace. The minister and all who are present embrace the dying Christian. In this and in other parts of the celebration the sense of leave-taking need not be concealed or denied, but the joy of Christian hope, which is the comfort and strength of the one near death, should also be evident."[28]

The dying person and all who are present may receive communion under both kinds. The sign of communion is more complete when received in this manner because it expresses more fully and clearly the nature of the eucharist as a meal, one which prepares all who take part in it for the heavenly banquet.

"The sick who are unable to receive under the form of bread may receive under the form of wine alone."[29]

"It often happens that a person who has received the eucharist as viaticum lingers in a grave condition or at the point of death for a period of days or longer. In these circumstances he or she should be given the opportunity to receive the eucharist as viaticum on successive days, frequently if not daily."[30]

In the rite of viaticum itself, there are appropriate prayers, readings, and blessings which underscore the notion of preparing the dying for the journey to eternity.

In addition to viaticum with its accompanying prayers and readings, Part II of the ritual, "Pastoral Care of the Dying," also contains a section called the commendation for the dying. Through it the Church helps to sustain the dying person's union with Christ in his passage out of this world to the Father until it is brought to fulfillment in death.[31]

The commendation of the dying includes appropriate prayers, litanies, aspirations, psalms, and biblical readings which "are intended to help the dying person, if still conscious, to face the natural human anxiety about death by imitating Christ in his patient suffering and dying. The Christian will be helped to surmount his or her fear in the hope of heavenly life and resurrection through the power of Christ, who destroyed the power of death by his own dying.

"Even if the dying person is not conscious, those who are present will draw consolation from these prayers and come to a better understanding of the paschal character of Christian death. This may be visibly expressed by making the sign of the cross on the forehead of the dying person, who was first signed with the cross at baptism."[32]

More and more Catholic parishes are developing a corps of volunteer persons who are comfortable with the thought of their own deaths, knowledgeable about the stages of dying, aware of the importance of listening and touching, familiar with the Church's special prayers for the dying, and willing to spend time by the bedside of a critically ill person.[33] By speaking words of comfort into the ear of failing individuals and by being present to them physically through such gestures as the Sign of the Cross traced on the forehead, these volunteers give courage and hope to the dying person. They also serve to underscore the truth that death is the final healing of this life's hurts. Christ never fails to heal us through the sacraments of anointing and viaticum: sometimes physically, always spiritually and—at our deaths—perfectly.

Discussion Questions

1. Identify in your mind five people you know or have heard about who at this moment are hurting from a physical or emotional pain.
2. Glance through the gospel according to Mark or Luke and notice how many times it describes Jesus healing someone. Then, look up the three texts in which Christ bestowed the power to heal upon the twelve apostles, the seventy-two disciples, and all who believe or profess faith in his name.
3. What are some of the ways we use oil today and some ways oil was employed during Christ's time?
4. Describe the general purpose of the anointing sacrament in the first eight hundred years, from the ninth through the sixteenth

centuries, and from the Council of Trent until the Second Vatican Council of our times.

5. Do you recall hearing anyone speak about the "last rites" of the Church? Why has the sacrament been called that? Is it appropriate? What does the Church call this rite today? Why?
6. List the overall and the three specific effects of this sacrament.
7. The sacrament of anointing is for those whose health is "seriously impaired." What persons would fall into that category and be eligible for the sacrament?
8. What are the essential elements in the ritual for the anointing of the sick?
9. How are many Catholic parishes in our time attempting to provide Holy Communion on a frequent, even daily and especially Sunday basis for the sick?
10. The Church provides viaticum and special prayers for the dying. Explain both and describe what creative efforts are being made in some churches to make these available for every critically ill person.

MATRIMONY:

building the little church

7

Matrimony: Building the Little Church

While all sacraments have a public or communal dimension, the five we have discussed up to this point—baptism, confirmation, the Eucharist, penance, and anointing of the sick—have in a sense an individual orientation.

Through baptism I am welcomed into the Church. At confirmation I receive the Holy Spirit in a unique way. In Communion I eat the Lord's Body and drink his Blood. With penance I am reconciled to the Lord, the Church, and others. By the anointing of the sick, I am strengthened to bear my burden bravely.

There are two other sacraments, however, which while naturally ministered to or received by individuals, have in a sense a public or communal purpose. One, matrimony, preserves the human race; the other, holy orders, perpetuates the Church.

Through their union in love, husband and wife have the possibility of creating new life and bringing forth children which will carry on humanity until the end. Through ordination, deacons, priests, and bishops officially preside over the sacraments, preach the Word, direct the Church, and empower others to be their successors, thus carrying on the Church until the final times.

Jesus and Marriage

Men and women, from Adam and Eve to Mary and Joseph, were

marrying before Jesus came into the world. Christ thus did not establish marriage, but he did show a unique regard for the joining of husband and wife, spoke a few significant words about that union, and elevated this natural relationship to the divine sacrament of matrimony. However, it took the Church a long time to develop a clear understanding about these matters or at least to express that comprehension explicitly. Even today there exists considerable confusion about the meaning of the Lord's words on marriage.

Jesus' initial miracle occurred during a wedding at Cana in Galilee. He took six stone jars filled to the brim with water and changed the water into choice wine, thus eliminating a potential moment of humiliation or embarrassment for the bridegroom and his family who had responsibility for the festal celebration. [1] John's Gospel concludes the incident with these words: "Jesus performed this first of his signs at Cana in Galilee. Thus did he reveal his glory, and his disciples believed in him" (2:11). Many would cite the fact that Christ began his miraculous deeds at a wedding feast as a sign of his particular interest in and blessing upon marriage.

The Master also made some specific comments about the unbreakability of the marital bond, words which sharply challenged the prevailing Jewish view of the day. Luke's Gospel contains Jesus' apodictic, unqualified, and straightforward statement: "Everyone who divorces his wife and marries another commits adultery. The man who marries a woman divorced from her husband likewise commits adultery" (16:18). Mark's Gospel includes the same prohibition of divorce in the context of an exchange with the Pharisees. In that discussion Christ added these famous words which represent the ideal and his teaching: "At the beginning of creation God made them male and female; for this reason a man shall leave his father and mother and the two shall become as one. They are no longer two but one flesh. Therefore let no man separate what God has joined" (10:6-9).

Most if not all Scripture scholars today maintain that these were Christ's original words, that he said divorce was wrong, that God did not have divorce in the divine plan, that the Lord judged it falling far short of moral perfection, and that this teaching radically departed from the traditional Jewish acceptance of divorce. [2]

What muddies matters here are two passages in Matthew's Gospel which have Jesus repeating that doctrine and exchange, but in both cases adding an exception. Divorce is not permitted, Christ says, except in cases of "lewd conduct" (5:31-32; 19:3-9).

The original Greek word of which "lewd conduct" is one trans-

lation possesses a variety of meanings. It can and has also been trans-
lated as "immorality," "incest," "adultery," "fornication," etc.
Scholars debate its precise meaning, but most would not restrict
its meaning to adultery alone. [3]

Students of Scripture and theologians tend to resolve this confusion by maintaining that Matthew's Gospel in its present form
was written later, around the year 80. It was, they hold, composed
in final fashion by someone other than the Apostle Matthew, who
added the exception clause to soften Jesus' teaching and bring it
in harmony with the practice of the early Jewish Christian community which allowed divorce in certain circumstances. It appears
certain that at least some Christians permitted divorce for special
reasons during the time the Gospels were written. [4]

The Church and Marriage

When Colleen McVey and Tony Griffo, whom we met in the first
chapter, prepared for their wedding ceremony a few years ago, they
first had to complete substantial paper work both for the secular
government (blood test, license) and the Catholic Church (secure
baptismal records, fill out a lengthy questionnaire).

If they had married during the first ten centuries or so of Christianity, Colleen and Tony would have found that there were no
Church requirements in this regard and that the secular state
handled all marriage and divorce details. Only with the breakdown
of civil society throughout the last part of the initial millenium did
the Church enter this picture. However, by the year 1000, as a consequence, all European marriages in effect came under Church
jurisdiction.

Nor would Tony and Colleen have been expected to follow a
specific religious ritual. An obligatory church ceremony began to
emerge only in the eleventh century and while by the twelfth century there was an established church wedding ceremony in different parts of Europe, numerous local variations kept this from being
a standard rite. [5]

With its growing involvement in both the legal and ceremonial
dimensions of marriage, the Church during that period reflected
upon and clarified several issues: the sacramental nature of marriage, divorce, and the required ceremony.

Within the twelfth and thirteenth centuries, Church leaders began to view marriage as one of the seven official sacraments. [6] This
doctrine of matrimony as a sacrament subsequently was formally

proclaimed at the Council of Florence (1439) and more explicitly defined at the Council of Trent (1563).[7]

In the twelfth century the Church came to a position absolutely prohibiting divorce based on canonical, sacramental, and theological reasons. That was likewise reinforced by the Council of Trent.[8]

At the same Council of Trent, to counteract harm caused by secret or clandestine marriages, the Church took a drastic step and declared: no Christian marriage would be valid or a sacrament unless contracted in the presence of a priest and two witnesses; those who did not follow this step would be judged guilty of grave sin and treated as adulterers; moreover, the forthcoming marriage had to be announced publicly three weeks in advance and registered in the parish records immediately afterwards.[9]

That official teaching on those three points has remained in effect over the subsequent centuries and continues to be Church policy, with some exceptions to be explained later, in our day.

The Wedding Ceremony Today

Prior to the Second Vatican Council Catholic nuptial celebrations had a fixed and clerical character to them. They were fixed in that the ritual, the readings, and other texts never varied. For example, the rite always included St. Paul's admonitions to the Ephesians in chapter 5 and Matthew's account of the exchange between Jesus and the Pharisees. They were clerical in that the priest did almost everything during the ceremony itself.

All of this changed radically in 1969. Commissioned to revise the rite of marriage, a group of international experts prepared a renewed version, which was ultimately authorized by Pope Paul VI in that year.[10]

The new ritual contains a rich variety of biblical readings, prayers, and blessings from which to choose and encourages the bride and groom to select those texts which best correspond to their hopes for the future. It provides other options for the celebration and urges the involvement of lay persons as leaders in the rite, such as lectors or readers. Finally, it stresses full congregational participation in the liturgy by word, song, and deed.

This approach has enjoyed an enthusiastic response from engaged couples.[11] In a personalist age most welcome the opportunity to prepare a celebration that is uniquely their own. The fact that bride and groom will spend hours in preparation for the nuptial service is a welcome contrast to former days when the bridal pair spent their time over details of the reception and the clergy cared for all elements of the church ceremony. That new system of preparing has obvious value in terms of fostering a deeper spiritual awareness about matrimony within the man and woman about to receive this sacrament.

The Sacrament

In our discussions to this point, the priest or bishop has been the minister of the sacrament and he does so with words, gestures, and material elements such as the water at baptism or the bread and wine for the Eucharist. In the sacrament of matrimony, however, all of that changes.

The revised approach stresses that the bride and groom minister the sacrament to one another; the priest (or deacon) simply serves as the Church's witness. Moreover, the essential element is not the pouring of water with accompanying words or the proclamation of a formula over bread and wine, but the matrimonial consent between baptized persons. Through that consent a man and a woman, through an irrevocable covenant, mutually give and accept each other in a partnership for the whole of life, a relationship designed both for the good of the spouses through their close, special unity and for the procreation and education of offspring. [12]

The sacrament, then, is the mutual promise and the living out of that commitment for life. This means that the Lord becomes present through grace in a new and deeper way at the moment of the exchange itself. But this also implies that Christ will continue to be present in a unique way whenever husband and wife carry out those mutual promises—whenever they serve one another, make love together, forgive each other, or reach out to others, including and especially their children. Finally, this likewise suggests that the couple can count on particular actual graces from time to time, which will assist them in fulfilling their responsibilities "in good times and in bad, in sickness and in health." [13]

A Covenant

The significant words in the above comments about the sacrament of matrimony is "irrevocable covenant." The Church today views marriage not so much a contract involving rights and obligations between husband and wife as a covenant of love between two persons mirroring the love covenant between God and us. A covenant involves a giving-receiving-responding exchange or agreement. The give and take between husband and wife is hard to define or totally understand even by the married couple themselves. It has an element of mystery to it.

The Vatican Council Fathers spoke of the family as a "little" or "domestic" Church, a mirror of the larger Church.[14] When we examine matrimony from a covenant and domestic Church perspective, these kind of comparisons or statements about the sacrament emerge:

- It is parallel to the covenant between God and the Chosen People described in the Hebrew Scriptures.
- It mirrors the marriage between God and humanity in Christ, the union of the divine and the human in Jesus.
- It reflects the new covenant between God and the People of God in Jesus Christ.
- It is a mystery, like the Church and related to the Church, which points to, leads beyond, and communicates something more than we immediately perceive with our senses. Thus, the love of Christ for the Church models the kind of love spouses are called to show for one another. Conversely, the love they experience with each other will lead husband and wife better to grasp the love God has for the Church and for us.
- It possesses a community dimension which reminds the couple that they travel through life not alone and unaided but surrounded by caring Christian people who will stand by them in their sorrows and share with them their joys.
- It places a responsibility upon husband and wife to reach out in love for those who are needy in any way and can benefit from their assistance.[15]

Preparing for the Sacrament

It should not prove surprising that the Church, considering the sacrament's dignity, its lifetime promises, contemporary society's disregard for long term commitments and today's high divorce rates, should insist upon careful preparations for the sacrament's celebration.

The ritual admonishes priests to "first of all strengthen and nourish the faith of those about to be married, for the sacrament of matrimony presupposes and demands faith."[16]

The new Code of Canon Law establishes similar regulations. It requires pastors of souls to offer assistance by providing among other things, "personal preparation for entering marriage so that through such preparation the parties may be predisposed toward the holiness and duties of their new state." It also urges them to facilitate "a fruitful liturgical celebration of marriage clarifying that spouses signify and share in that mystery of unity and of fruitful love that exists between Christ and the Church." [17]

The Vatican Council document on lay people explicitly noted that the laity should work at "assisting engaged couples to make a better preparation for marriage." [18]

Those admonitions have been taken seriously in the United States. A wide variety of pre-marriage or pre-Cana programs, courses, or conferences exist around the country. Some involve a one-to-one or couple-to-couple session or series of sessions between a "veteran" married couple and the engaged pair. Others assemble a group of engaged couples for a day or several evenings and feature presentations, plus discussions by married couples and experts on marital life. A third variation called Engaged Encounter gathers a cluster of engaged for one weekend at a retreat setting directed by a priest and married couples who explore together with some intensity key issues about marriage. In addition, there are combinations of the above, plus the individual conferences between the parish priest and the engaged couple.

While some clergy have taken a rather strict attitude toward couples who seek a church wedding for more social than religious reasons, Pope John Paul II, in a commentator's summary of his words, urges that "if only a shred of evidence indicates openness on the part of the couple, the Church community should grasp that and welcome the couple into its presence." [19] The preparation and celebration thus should attempt to strengthen and nourish what may appear to be a weak and underdeveloped faith.

Interfaith Marriages

In the 1940s after the death of my father, my Roman Catholic mother entered a second marriage with a conscientious Episcopalian. They exchanged their vows in the rectory of our small town parish church.

In the 1950s my brother took as his bride a young lady with a Protestant tradition. They made their nuptial promises in a Catholic church but outside the sanctuary.

In the 1960s, during the initial years of my priesthood, I officiated at many "mixed" or "interfaith" marriages, but these took place within the sanctuary.

In the 1970s, the situation further shifted so that such weddings between a Catholic and one not Roman Catholic might include a nuptial Mass and blessing, possibilities previously reserved for occasions when both were Roman Catholic.

This gradual change represents the Church's attempt to balance two pastoral concerns: the Church wishes to encourage marital unions in which both share the same faith and religious practice, but it also wishes to show great solicitude for the many couples who will enter interfaith marriages.

While some view a mixed or interfaith marriage as a means toward building Christian unity and overcoming the separation between Christian traditions, most would judge the religious differences as a serious challenge to the success of the union and the preservation or deepening of the couple's faith.[20] Those bitter scenes in the musical *Fiddler on the Roof* during which the Jewish father rejects, even considers dead his daughter who has married a non-Jew dramatizes the pain of this dilemma in which love and faith conflict.

Since January 1, 1971, the Catholic Church in the United States, applying to this country norms or guidelines for mixed marriages issued by Pope Paul VI, offers much greater flexibility for the engaged "mixed" couple, one Catholic and the other not, who wish to marry. For example:

- They may have the banns or announcements of the forthcoming marriage published in advance.
- As noted above, they may celebrate their vows in the context of a nuptial Mass.
- The non-Catholic's minister is welcomed to participate in the ceremony.
- The person who is not Catholic signs no statement and makes no promises about the Catholic upbringing of the children.
- The Catholic signs or gives orally this promise: "I reaffirm my faith in Jesus Christ and, with God's help, intend to continue living that faith in the Catholic Church. I promise to do all in my power to share the faith I have received with our children by having them baptized and reared as Catholics." The non-Catholic spouse needs to be aware of this promise.
- With the bishop's permission the marriage may take place in the church of the person who is not a Catholic and be witnessed by the clergy of that tradition.[21]

While these more flexible procedures do not resolve the challenging differences, particularly in the religious upbringing of children, they have eliminated many previously painful situations and enabled Catholic clergy to deal more positively with the many inter-faith couples which increasingly emerge in our pluralistic society.

Divorce and Remarriage

Some Catholic theologians, examining the exception clauses in St. Matthew's Gospel mentioned above and the interpretation that early Christians softened Jesus' strict teaching on divorce, argue for the possibility of remarriage after divorce. [22]

However, official Catholic teaching continues to uphold the absolute prohibition of remarriage after divorce. [23]

If that is so, what happens then when a Catholic marriage breaks up? How do we explain the increasing number of Roman Catholics in second marriages with the presumed blessing of the Church?

First, we should observe that the Church does not prohibit civil separation, divorce, or annulment actions. Catholics who secure these do not lose their good standing in the Church and thus are free to receive the sacraments. In fact, more and more parishes, regions, or dioceses have groups, agencies, or persons seeking to offer personal counseling and spiritual support for those who have or are suffering the death of that nuptial bond and relationship.

Remarriage after divorce, however, is a different issue. Quite simply, for that to take place in the Catholic Church, the previously married person(s) must secure an ecclesiastical declaration of nullity or annulment for that earlier union(s), unless, of course, the former spouse has died. Since the Church presumes all marriages are valid unless proven otherwise, that includes, and this is a surprise to many, persons who are not Roman Catholic and were married civilly or before a minister of another tradition.

Some of these declarations of nullity are relatively uncomplicated. For example, when a Catholic was not married before a priest, documented proof of that fact will generally be sufficient to secure the needed annulment prior to a second marriage.

Some are more complex and involve a formal procedure. Fortunately, beginning in 1970 the process for such annulments was streamlined and the reasons sufficient for the declaration of nullity were greatly expanded. [24] They include: "lack of discretion (the parties did not really understand what they were committing themselves to), lack of partnership in conjugal life, lack of conjugal love, psychopathic personality, schizophrenia, affective immaturity, psychic incompetence, sociopathic personality, 'moral impotence,' lack of interpersonal communication." [25]

The simplified steps and expanded grounds have resulted in a rapid increase in the number of Church annulments throughout the United States. This has brought relief and hope to many who experienced the tragedy of a failed marriage and wished to begin again. It has also engendered confusion and even resentment among others who wonder why and how Catholics can now marry after divorce.

The Church here is trying to pursue a middle course of upholding the permanence of the marriage bond while providing an opportunity for remarriage to those whose initial marital union from the beginning lacked an essential ingredient.

* * *

Several Saturdays ago on a morning and afternoon I participated in two wedding celebrations. The first took place in a Methodist church with the bride of that tradition and the groom a Roman Catholic. Her minister and I shared in the non-Eucharistic service which included elements from both of our Churches' rituals selected by the couple. The second, between two Catholics, took place at the cathedral within the context of a nuptial Mass and included prayers, readings, and blessings chosen in advance by the engaged pair. Friends proclaimed the readings; relatives brought forth the gifts; many received Holy Communion.

The fact that the interfaith celebration could be held in her Methodist church with the blessing of the Catholic bishop, the fact that both couples spent hours during courtship preparing nuptial liturgies, and the fact that several, even all took an active part in the wedding services brought joy to many, deepened the participants' appreciation for the sacrament of matrimony, and gave the two couples a fine send-off on their life-long journeys.

In the years ahead, each pair will be building their relationship, their home and their family into a little or domestic church, a miniature and mirror of the larger Church.

Discussion Questions

1. If you were to divide the seven sacraments into two categories, how would you do so? What would be the reason behind each category?
2. Jesus showed his high regard for marriage and his strong views about divorce. How did he manifest that regard and what did he say about divorce?

3. Since the Council of Trent, official Church teaching on marriage has generally speaking maintained three points. What are they?

4. Compare a Catholic wedding ceremony prior to the Second Vatican Council and those commonplace in the United States since 1969.

5. What is the essential element of the ritual for the sacrament of matrimony, and what are the effects of this sacrament for the married couple?

6. The Church today views matrimony as a covenant of love between two people more than a contract of rights and obligations between spouses. Think of some married people you know who seem to be living out that covenant very well and describe how they appear to be carrying out the full meaning of such a covenant in their lives.

7. How would you respond to a Catholic couple who have seldom been at Sunday Mass and seem almost indifferent to the Church but now contact their parish and seek a typically "large" and formal Catholic Church wedding?

8. Do you judge "living together" is an appropriate preparation for marriage? Why or why not?

9. Describe how Catholic regulations about interfaith marriages have changed in the past few decades and what are the current directives about them.

10. Explain to an interested inquirer how a Catholic, married for a number of years and parent of several children, could get a divorce and remarry in the Catholic Church with official approval.

HOLY ORDERS:

continuing the larger church

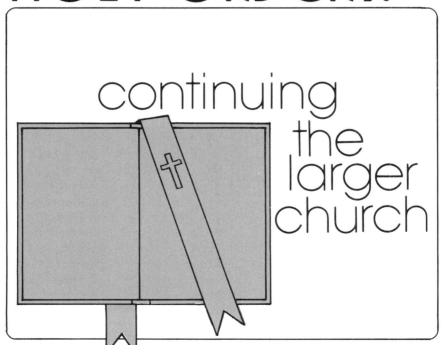

8

Holy Orders: Continuing the Larger Church

My ordination to the priesthood in February 1956 culminated nearly a decade of study and formation following high school graduation. It also was the last stage in a series of rituals leading to, connected with, and involving the sacrament of holy orders.

Early in the last four years of preparation, the presiding bishop clipped a section of my hair during the rite of tonsure, and I along with forty-eight classmates officially became a cleric, an individual set aside to do the Lord's work in a unique way.

Over the next few years we received four minor orders—porter, lector, exorcist, and acolyte—also from the hands of the local bishop. These designated us as persons caring for the church building, reading the Scriptures, casting out devils, and serving at the altar. In point of fact we had been performing most of those functions already, and the reception of these titles or powers meant little outside the seminary walls and not much to us inside them other than as additional steps covered on our journey to the priesthood.

At the beginning of the final year, we became subdeacons and at that ordination ritual pledged ourselves to life-long celibacy and daily praying of the divine office or breviary. Shortly thereafter the bishop returned and we received the diaconate, empowered by the Church now to preach, baptize, assist at the altar, and distribute Communion. While the other rituals were called ordinations and the gifts bestowed through them known as orders, the diaconate was the first one considered a sacrament in the strict sense of the word. Even so, as deacons we exercised these ministries on relatively few occasions and knew that it was only a transitional diaconate, another and last formal ceremony and stage prior to the great day when we would become priests.

Ordination Today

For those ordained to the priesthood today, the training, the steps, and the ordination ritual are radically different. The formation still requires eight or nine years after high school, but following the directives of the Second Vatican Council and subsequent documents, both the content of courses and the style or approach have been altered, updated, and adjusted to modern situations. [1]

The steps were revised by Pope Paul VI in 1972. The Holy Father dropped tonsure and established instead a ceremony for entrance into the clerical state connected with the diaconate. He also eliminated the four minor orders and called them instead "ministries," now open to laymen and not reserved to candidates for the sacrament of orders. Moreover, Paul VI preserved the ministries of reader and acolyte for the whole Church, but suppressed the major order of subdiaconate. Finally, the Pope restored an older form of the diaconate, making this sacrament available to men, including those already married, as a permanent state and not merely as a transition on the way to the priesthood. [2]

The ordination ritual likewise has undergone modifications. Current rites for the ordination of deacons, priests, and bishops reflect the general liturgical reforms noted throughout this book. They more actively, for example, involve participants in the celebrations. In addition, Pope Paul VI precisely defined the essential elements of all three ordination ceremonies as the laying on of hands and the recitation by the bishop of a determined formula. [3] Those to be ordained to the priesthood at the present time, kneel, feel the bishop's hands laid upon their heads, then one after the other the hands of all priests present, and eventually hear these consecratory words:

> Almighty Father,
> grant to these servants of yours
> the dignity of the priesthood.
> Renew within them the Spirit of holiness.
> As co-workers with the order of bishops

may they be faithful to the ministry
that they receive from you, Lord God,
and be to others a model of right conduct. [4]

The Early Days of Ordination

We have traditionally held that Jesus instituted the priesthood on Holy Thursday at the Last Supper when Christ told the apostles to "do this as a remembrance of me" (Luke 22:19). [5]

Scholars today continue to maintain that our Lord explicitly instituted the Eucharist at this Holy Thursday event. [6] However, contemporary Church historians and Scripture experts question the express institution by Christ of the priesthood at the Last Supper. [7] They would hold instead that Jesus implied the establishment of the sacraments by his teaching on the Kingdom, but left it to the Church under the Holy Spirit to develop all of them, including holy orders later in the history of Christianity. [8]

Nevertheless, by the end of the first century, Christian writers compared Jesus' death on the cross to a priestly sacrifice and within a short period there emerged persons who presided over the Eucharistic celebrations much in the fashion of Jewish priests. [9]

In a relatively brief time, by the beginning of the second century, we read about a rather clearly defined hierarchy of local leaders—bishops, presbyters, and deacons—in the letters of St. Ignatius of Antioch. Their task was to maintain order in the Church, an order which included doctrine, worship, and behavior, as well as an order which established a new relationship between God and humans in the Church. Hence the term "holy orders." These ordained persons possessed authority and others in the community were expected to be submissive to them. [10]

As early as around A.D. 215 the directives or rubrics accompanying the ordination ritual contained in the classic *Apostolic Tradition* of Hippolytus says this about deacons and their relation to priests and bishops:

> And when a deacon is ordained . . . . the bishop alone shall lay on hands, because he is not being ordained to the priesthood, but to the service of the bishop . . . . For he does not share in the counsel of the presbyterate, but administers and informs the bishop of what is fitting; he does not receive the common spirit of seniority in which the presbyters share, but that which is entrusted to him under the bishop's authority. [11]

Over succeeding centuries we can note these developments: the permanent diaconate disappeared; the various minor orders arose as described at the beginning of this chapter; holy orders came in the middle ages to be viewed as one of the seven sacraments; official Church ministries were done almost exclusively by the ordained clergy; the idea of the sacrament's permanent character, first conceived by Augustine, was revived by twelfth-century theologians and became the standard teaching of the Church.[12]

Pope Paul VI's decrees and the decisions of the Second Vatican Council thus both restore certain elements of holy orders operative in the earliest years of Christianity, but also provide the possibility for future evolutions. We will look at the latter in a moment.

Grace and Functions

The individual deacon, priest, or bishop receives, as in the other sacraments, a deepening of Christ's life within him through sanctifying grace. Moreover, he can depend upon actual graces to provide wisdom and strength to carry out the responsibilities of his new office throughout life. In addition, holy orders, like baptism and confirmation, is seen as somehow communicating a character which permanently designates the recipient as a deacon, priest, or bishop.[13]

That permanent character raises several practical pastoral difficulties. If one is ordained, for example, as a "priest forever according to the order of Melchisedech," what occurs in these situations: When a priest or bishop resigns from the active ministry to enter a new life-style? When an ordained person is prohibited by the bishop or pope from carrying out his functions because of scandalous behavior or other inadequacies? When, as some suggest, the Church might introduce a practice of temporary commitment to the priesthood, for example, allowing a person to serve for a term of five or ten years?

The sacrament of holy orders not only bestows those graces and that character; it also formally sets aside a person for specific functions in the Church.

"The deacon is called to serve the People of God in the ministry of the liturgy, of the word and of charity."[14] Deacons, permanent and transitional, thus today assist the presiding priest or bishop at the altar, baptize, witness marriages, conduct funerals, preach, teach, and normally engage in some activity or several activities to help the hurting.

The priest, in addition to his role as teacher and leader, is designated as a presider over worship. In that capacity he can celebrate most of the sacraments. While the deacon also ministers some, as noted above, only the priest at the present offers Mass, grants absolution in the sacrament of penance, and anoints the sick.

The bishop possesses all the graces and designations of deacon and priest, but in addition he may ordain deacons and priests and is the ordinary minister of confirmation.

In a sense, therefore, holy orders insures the continuation of the larger Church, since it regularly sets aside persons who will preside over the Eucharist, which is the summit or source of the Church's life and minister as well the other sacraments.

There are, however, several current developments and issues connected with holy orders which need to be discussed, even if briefly.

Ministry of the Baptized

As we have noted, in earliest days baptized Christians took an active part in the life of the Church, performing a variety of tasks and fulfilling many ministries. With the emergence of a defined priesthood and other "orders," that soon disappeared and the most significant functions were carried out by ordained persons.

The Second Vatican Council officially sought to reverse this practice. Its documents stressed that through the initiation sacraments of baptism, confirmation, and the Eucharist each member shares in the priesthood of Christ. With this dignity goes the right and the responsibility of building up the Church. The Lord consequently appoints all those baptized and confirmed to share "in the salvific mission of the Church."[15]

During the past two decades there has been an enormous explosion of such lay ministries in the Church. Lay women and men carry out or assist with many functions formerly reserved exclusively to the clergy. Praiseworthy and valuable in itself, that remarkable growth has proven particularly helpful, even essential in view of the declining numbers of clergy through resignations, deaths, and decrease in vocations to the clerical state.

This theological shift and pastoral development understandably altered the role or function of the clergy. Still ministers of the Word and sacraments, they now also must serve as enablers and coordinators of the gifts which the baptized possess and share. It is for the clergy as leaders to facilitate processes which will achieve the following goals:

- identify needs in the Church;
- encourage people with appropriate gifts to come forward for service in response to those demands;
- train these volunteers or paid persons in the necessary skills;
- provide them with spiritual formation, guidance, and support;
- offer a vision of future possibilities;
- coordinate or unify the great diversity of efforts operating in the Church.

Some would parallel the clergy's leadership position today to that of a symphony conductor who plays some instruments, recognizes the value of all, and blends the entire body into one beautiful, harmonized sound. Others, half in jest and half in great seriousness, would instead parallel clergy to the ringmaster of a circus who links together many activities that are quite distinct and not closely related to one another.

Such a mushrooming of lay ministries has also brought new challenges through its resultant blurring of the clergy's identity and its creation of entirely new relationships between clergy and laity in the Church's life. A case in point concerns lectors and Communion ministers.

When Pope Paul VI instituted a permanent ministry for readers and acolytes in 1972, he reserved that institution "in accordance with the venerable tradition of the Church . . . to men."[16] In point of fact, men and women by the thousands have been proclaiming the Scriptures and assisting with the distribution of the Eucharist in the United States for many years. This restriction to men only therefore did not correspond to the pastoral scene in this country. As a result the institution of the permanent ministry of readers and acolytes has been almost universally ignored. Instead parishes or even dioceses conduct "commissioning ceremonies" whereby both female and male lectors or Communion ministers are formally designated for these functions, in most cases for a term of several years.

Something similar often occurs on the local level for other ministries like parish council members or religious education instructors.

Permanent Deacons

When Pope Paul VI restored the permanent diaconate in 1972, he opened the possibility of ordination both to unmarried men (must be at least twenty-five) and married men (must be at least thirty-five).[17] Many, but not all dioceses in the United States, quickly established formation programs and currently, less than a decade later, there are about six thousand active permanent deacons in this country.

They fulfill the deacon's liturgical and teaching roles in varying degrees depending on each one's particular work of service. Some, as their service work, have become full or part-time, paid or volunteer staff persons in parishes. Their liturgical and teaching role is to teach and preach in the parish, regularly assist at the Eucharist, minister Communion to the sick, baptize, officiate at weddings, and perhaps preside at some funeral rites.

Probably the majority have, as their service work, assumed personal responsibilities in a special location or unique field. For example, there are deacons who work with alcoholics, visit local jails, care for the spiritual needs of nursing home residents, assist hospital chaplains, supervise marriage preparation programs, and serve as business managers in diocesan offices. The liturgical and teaching dimension of their diaconate is either connected to that work or limited to weekend and festal occasions in their parishes.

Ideally the deacon is seen as a bridge between the secular world and the Church. Remaining very much part of the former, he officially represents and is permanently committed to ministry in the latter. Yet, the deacon's precise identity, the part a wife plays in this role, as well as the deacon's relationship to priests and parish life are areas still being clarified. The lack of clarity here has been a source of growing pains for all concerned.

Married Priests

There have always been and are now married Catholic priests with families who actively and with Church approval have fulfilled and do fulfill the priestly ministry, particularly in the Eastern rite as we will see below.

Nevertheless, from the earliest centuries there were movements which urged the clergy to follow a life of continence, perfect chastity, and celibacy. For example, during one of the sessions at the Council of Nicaea in the fourth century, some bishops proposed a new law requiring this. However, Paphnutius, himself a venerable and celibate bishop from Upper Egypt, argued against it, saying too heavy a yoke ought not to be laid upon the clergy.[18] Instead it would be enough, he maintained, to abide by the ancient tradition of the Church and forbid clerics to marry after ordination. His argument carried the day.[19]

The impetus continued, nevertheless, and various local councils in Rome and Carthage between 386–400 passed laws which enjoined continence upon all priests and deacons. That was for the Catholic Church in the West; the Catholic Church in the East maintained a different stance. In the East the practice remained: married and single men could be ordained deacons and priests; after ordination those single ones were not allowed to marry, nor widowed deacons or priests to remarry; finally, bishops in the East were required to be celibates.[20]

These local laws about a celibate clergy took on a universal dimension for the Catholic Church of the West through legislation during the First and Second Lateran Councils in the twelfth century. Those regulations about mandatory celibacy were reaffirmed by the Council of Trent in 1563. However, the bishops there clearly stated that this was an ecclesiastical, not a divine, mandate.[21]

Conscious of the human and therefore changeable aspect of the law mandating celibacy, many have proposed, especially in view of the growing contemporary clergy shortage, removal of that obligation for priests, making celibacy optional. Nevertheless, recent popes, including Pope John Paul II, have responded negatively to this suggestion and on the contrary supported the value of celibacy among priests for the Church in our day.[22]

At the same time, the Pope allowed in 1985 the bishop of Rochester, New York, to receive into the Church a Polish National Catholic priest, married and father of several, who then continued his priestly ministry in a Roman Catholic parish of that diocese. This exception was somewhat similar to other actions in recent years involving United States Episcopalian clergy embracing the Roman Catholic Church and followed parallel permissions granted earlier in Europe.

Ordination of Women

At the Detroit conference on the Liturgy in August 1985 a married woman and mother, active in her parish and even employed there part-time as a religious education coordinator for her parish, spoke to me after a lecture on alienation and reconciliation in the Church. Distraught and tearful, she described her rage and hopelessness over this issue of women's ordination. The questioner perceives the Church's specific refusal to ordain women and treatment of women in general as quite unjust.

Another woman, a suburban mother objecting to an article in a clerical journal which defended the prohibition against women's ordination, wrote with evident bitterness to the editor about the essay. In part she commented:

> I am appalled to think that in 1985 such garbage thinking still exists. I have two children, a son and a daughter, who are currently members of a local Catholic inner-city parish. One is no less qualified to study theology than the other since both are highly intelligent and sensitive humans. However, my daughter's eligibility is excluded from serious study for the priesthood because she is female. I find this kind of discriminatory treatment truly unjust . . . .
> I may not have the credentials which the author has but I possess parenting credentials which allow me the right to direct the thinking of children in a positive way and not a sexist way. [23]

The discussion about women's ordination is more complex than the matter of mandatory celibacy. There have been, are now, and surely will be in the future married Roman Catholic clergy in good standing who actively fulfill their ordained ministry. The Church could tomorrow make celibacy for priests optional. We are talking here about a human, ecclesiastical regulation, not a divinely given commandment.

We do not find, however, a similar tradition or history of ordained women in the Church. There were deaconesses in the early Church prior to the universal acceptance of clerical celibacy. These women were wives of bishops, priests, or deacons who shared in their husbands' ministries and facilitated their service. There were also women deacons ordained or ordered to the diaconate and serving in identical ways to men deacons. [24]

Nevertheless, "women were never ordained to priestly ministry, that is, to function as president or principal celebrant at the Eucharistic liturgy. Nor did women ever function as direct assistant at the celebration of the Eucharist. In other words, there is no evidence to support any claim that women were admitted to priesthood in the sense in which priesthood is understood today." [25]

Nor do we have any historical evidence of a woman bishop in the Church's two-thousand-year history.

One can thus rather easily justify the reintroduction of women deacons based on the Church's pattern of the past. But ordination of women priests or bishops?

Those, like the Detroit religious education coordinator or the suburban mother, who seek the ordination of women as priests and bishops argue that no biblical or theological reasons stand in the way of such a development in the Church. Moreover, they would maintain that Jesus and his Church never ordained women to these posts before because of purely cultural reasons, namely, the sexist attitudes over the centuries. Since that milieu has now changed, they would urge the Church to shift its position.

The official Church, on the other hand, considers this not merely as a disciplinary debate but a doctrinal discussion. Does the fact that no women have been ordained priests or deacons in its two millenia history reflect the mind of Christ or merely mirror the culture in which the Church has existed? If it reflects Jesus' will, the Church must be faithful to that and cannot alter its position. If it merely mirrors the culture, the Church could and probably would adjust its stand. The issue of women's ordination to priesthood or the episcopacy will not, as a consequence, be so easily resolved since it bears doctrinal overtones.

While the above analysis may accurately summarize the question at hand, I know from experience that such a delineation would do little to ease the rage or hurt of the conference participant, the New York mother, or others who push strongly for the ordination of women.

Who can predict how these different issues involving the sacrament of holy orders will be resolved as we end this century or head into the year 2000 and beyond? What we do know, however, is that Christ, promising to be with God's people until the end, will through the Spirit continue the larger Church in some fashion and the gates of hell shall not prevail against it.

Discussion Questions

1. What three persons have received the sacrament of holy orders?
2. Did Jesus specifically institute the priesthood at the Last Supper?
3. What is the meaning of "holy orders" and why do we call this sacrament by that name?
4. Three sacraments communicate a permanent character and thus are never repeated. Can you name them?
5. List some of the functions carried out by all ordained persons and which tasks are reserved to only one or two of the ordained.
6. The three initiation sacraments bestow on every Catholic Christian both the right and the responsibility to use her or his gift for building up the Church. What are those three sacraments? Give as many examples as you can of new roles being fulfilled by lay persons in the Church today which formerly were exclusively reserved to the clergy.

7. Some would term the priest's role today as one of a symphony conductor or a circus ring-master. Explain the meaning behind those titles.
8. Are you familiar with any permanent deacons in your area? Could you describe their functions and their purpose in the contemporary Church?
9. Sketch briefly the history of married priests in the Church and give your reasons why the Church of the West in most instances continues to require celibacy of its priests.
10. How would you summarize the current status of the issue about the ordination of women to the priesthood in the Catholic Church?

9

Sacramentals: Connecting the Creator and Creation

Fair weather visitors to the St. Lawrence River between Canada and upper New York State usually take a several hour boat trip around the spectacularly beautiful Thousand Islands. Sitting or standing on an open deck of their large tour vessel, these people cannot but be impressed by the natural magnificence of the surroundings. On the journey they will likewise occasionally pass by humanly made religious artifacts—a shrine honoring Mary, a statue of Christ, or a massive cross erected on a lofty ledge. During the trip they will hear from their guide of a past collision which sent an iron ore ship to the bottom of the swift-flowing river where it remains today with a multi-million dollar cargo and perhaps the bodies of some crew members who perished in the disaster.

Some Truths About Creation

That pleasant trip can communicate several truths about both creation and the Creator.

The power, wisdom, and goodness of an invisible God are made visible through the beauty of nature.

Genesis tells us that after creating the world, "God looked at everything he had made, and he found it very good" (Gen 1:31). Psalm 8 sings out "O Lord, our Lord, how glorious is your name over all the earth" (8:1). St. Paul severely warned the Romans about "irreligious" and "perverse" people who fail to recognize God through the created world around them. "These men are inexcusable," he says, because "since the creation of the world, invisible realities, God's eternal power and divinity, have become visible, recognized through the things he has made" (1:20).

Women and men have a need to express the deep and invisible sentiments of their hearts in visible ways.

We shake hands, kiss, salute a flag, send birthday cards, give Christmas presents, stand during the national anthem, pause before a grave, carry photographs of children or grandchildren, and go out for dinner on anniversaries. The list of examples has no end because in countless ways we use words, gestures, objects, time and space to speak of thoughts or feelings inside us.

That shrine to Mary, statue of Christ, or cross on the island top reflect this profound human need and desire to express visibly our invisible aspirations which understandably include religious sentiments.

Creation, despite its essential goodness and beauty, has often been disfigured by human actions and may even seem flawed because of those deeds. In a sense, the world around us or, more accurately, our perception and use of the world around us needs correction and ordering.

After the original sin or fall, the garden of paradise became a field of thorns and thistles (Gen 3:17). Still glorious, the created world appears wounded and in need of God's healing touch. One writer illustrates this contrast or conflict between the glorious and wounded aspect of nature through St. Francis of Assisi. That famous saint praised God's presence in the beauty surrounding him, called the earth his "brother," and named the moon his "sister." Yet each night he sang a Marian hymn which spoke of this life as a "valley of tears" and our home here as an "exile."[1]

The waters of the St. Lawrence can refresh swimmers, provide catch for those who fish, bring joy to boaters, and transport needed materials. But they have also brought death to many and form a watery grave for some.

Sacraments and Sacramentals

The Church has given us both sacraments and sacramentals to help in that healing process needed as it were to redeem creation, to modify our perception of nature, and to rectify our use of the world in which we live.

In the early Christian years the word "sacrament" was not precisely defined. Many things, in fact even all elements of the entire surrounding world, were seen as signs or sacraments speaking of God to us and making the Lord present in our midst. In time, however, that term became applied only to the rites we have examined in this book. At three medieval Church councils the number of sacraments was fixed at seven.[2]

Nevertheless, the Church continued even after those councils its practice of using words, actions, objects, time and space in special ways to facilitate exchanges between the invisible God and earth-bound humans. Called sacramentals, the recent Code of Canon Law defined them in this way: "Somewhat in the imitation of the sacraments, sacramentals are sacred signs by which spiritual effects are signified and are obtained by the intercession of the Church."[3]

That definition grew out of these following statements about the nature and purpose of sacramentals made by the bishops at the Second Vatican Council:

> Holy Mother Church has, moreover, instituted sacramentals. These are sacred signs which bear a resemblance to the sacraments. They signify effects, particularly of a spiritual nature, which are obtained through the Church's intercession. By them men are disposed to receive the chief effect of the sacraments, and various occasions in life are rendered holy.

> Thus, for well-disposed members of the faithful the liturgy of the sacraments and sacramentals sanctifies almost every event of their lives with the divine grace which flows from the paschal mystery of the Passion, Death and Resurrection of Christ. From this source all sacraments and sacramentals draw their power. There is scarcely any proper use of material things which cannot thus be directed toward the sanctification of men and the praise of God.[4]

The comparisons below may help in understanding the difference between the sacraments and sacramentals.

- There are seven sacraments; there are an unlimited and nearly countless number of sacramentals.
- The sacraments are fixed in number; sacramentals can disappear when no longer pastorally useful, and new ones may be added as different spiritual needs develop.
- The sacraments have carefully delineated essential elements; the sacramentals by their nature may be any formula, object, action, time or space which the Church now or in the future "blesses" for a special religious purpose.

- The sacraments cause grace primarily through a God-given inherent power in the rite itself (*ex opere operato* is the classical Latin term for this); the sacramentals do so primarily through the faith and devotion of those who are using, receiving and celebrating the sacramental (*ex opere operantis* is the Latin for this).
- The sacraments more specifically were instituted by Christ, although, in some instances as we have seen, through the later indirect instrumentality of the Church; the sacramentals have been, are, and will be more directly established by the Church. [5]

Some Examples

There are what we might term informal sacramentals used by believers as an expression of faith, but which do not have a distinct Church blessing. A man might tip his hat passing a church or a woman (in former days) cover her head entering one; parents may lay their hands in blessing upon a child; visitors to religious shrines may follow traditions of climbing stairs on their knees, taking special baths, or touching particular statues.

What we might call formal sacramentals, those fitting the definition and description above, require a Church "blessing" by an authorized person and according to an approved rite or formula. [6]

Here are some illustrations of well-known Catholic sacramentals:

- *Words and Actions:* The Sign of the Cross; a bow or genuflection before altar or tabernacle; processions around and outside the church; blessing of a new car, boat, or house.
- *Objects:* Candles used in worship or prayer; ashes at the beginning of Lent and palms before Holy Week; crucifixes; statues, paintings and stained glass representations of saints or holy people; incense; religious medals.
- *Time:* Sundays; Christmas, Easter, Pentecost, Christ the King and other feasts re-presenting the major events in Jesus' life; celebrations of saints; Advent, Lent, and the Easter seasons; holy hours of adoration; special days of prayer, fasting and abstinence.
- *Space:* Churches and chapels; rooms for reconciliation or penance; retreat centers; shrines at noted locations (e.g., Holy Land, Lourdes, Fatima, Assisi).

Past Practice and Needed Revision

Prior to the Second Vatican Council, the Latin Roman Ritual contained not only the appropriate rites for the sacraments but also blessings for an enormous number of sacramentals. The index of an English version, for example, lists in consecutive order, among others, a blessing of "barn, beer, bees, bell, betrothal, birds, blast-furnace, boat, bonfire, bread, bridal-chamber, brick-kiln, bridge, butter."[7]

Priests sometimes employed a few of these blessing texts, but most of those rites remained merely a part of that book without ever being used. In addition, many objects like medals, rosaries, crucifixes, Bibles, or prayer books were blessed by the clergy with a simple Sign of the Cross and perhaps a sprinkling with holy water. Sacramentals of the formal kind generally were not used to the extent possible nor celebrated in the most productive manner.

This led the Council Fathers to state: "With the passage of time, however, there have crept into the rites of the sacraments and sacramentals certain features which have rendered their nature and purpose far from clear to the people of today. Hence some changes are necessary to adapt them to present-day needs."[8]

More specifically they directed that in these revisions or changes the primary principle to be kept in mind should be modifications which would enable the faithful to participate in the sacramentals "intelligently, actively and easily." In addition, the reformers should consider the circumstances of our times and add new sacramentals as necessity requires. They also indicated that under special circumstances qualified lay persons may administer the blessings or sacramentals, a function formerly reserved exclusively to priests.[9]

Current Developments

During the two decades while Church officials have been implementing those directions and developing a revised book of blessings, several liturgical leaders in the United States have both studied this issue and created a temporary text of new blessings.

Fr. Lawrence Brett sees a number of steps necessary if sacramentals are to have the spiritual impact which the Church desires. In his judgment these are: the need always to have readings from scripture whenever celebrating a sacramental; the need for a clear connection between the blessing rite and the world around us; the need to have clear, full and simple signs in the sacramental ritual (water should flow, oil ooze, clothing drape); the need to have the community, at least in the form of some representative believers, present for the celebration; the need to create new and additional sacramentals which meet the demands of our times.[10]

Thomas Simons has not only studied the question of blessings in depth, but also produced an interim book of blessings, which fulfills some of the needs outlined by Father Brett.[11]

His "Blessing of a Vehicle," to illustrate, goes beyond a single prayer, Sign of the Cross, and sprinkling with holy water. It includes a call to worship, reading of Scripture, intercessions, and blessing prayer. The rite involves lay persons actively and relates the ritual to daily life.

Petitions of the Intercessions mention: "Father, bless all who use this car (truck, boat, these vehicles). May they be conscious of their responsibility toward others . . . . Help us to avoid all danger and accident by our carefulness . . . . Protect us from harm and bring us back home in peace and joy."

A concluding suggestion reads: "Bless the vehicle(s) with holy water, if desired. Families may want to place an image of Christ in their vehicle as a sign of dedication and a reminder of the Lord's presence and blessing."[12]

Tomorrow's Blessings

In 1984 Pope John Paul II issued the revised Book of Blessings in its Latin edition. Liturgical scholars and pastoral leaders are, at this writing, currently preparing both an English translation of that text and adaptations of it to the needs of our country.

The renewed ritual of blessings will, of course, follow the general Vatican II directives noted above. This includes provision for some sacramentals to be administered by lay persons who are endowed with the appropriate qualities.[13]

In light of that possibility, one expert envisions a future of newly created blessings and of circumstances in which "parents would bless their children, and preside at the blessing of an engaged couple. Workers and technicians, the tools of their trade and expertise. Farmers and ranchers, their fields and livestock. The caring, their sick and befriended. Hosts, their guests. Teachers, their students."[14]

The Vatican Council Fathers began the Pastoral Constitution on the Church in the Modern World with these now oft-quoted words: "the joy and hope, the grief and anguish" of people in our time, "especially of those who are poor or afflicted in any way, are the joy and hope, the grief and anguish of the followers of Christ as well. Nothing that is genuinely human fails to find an echo in their hearts."[15]

The sacramentals are powerful vehicles for bringing all human joy, hope, grief, and anguish under the influence of Christ's healing grace. They can help clarify our vision of creation, correct our weaknesses, and connect us with the loving Creator of heaven and earth.

Discussion Questions

1. What particular beauties of nature speak to you about God?
2. Indicate several ways in which you have recently expressed the deep and invisible sentiments of your heart in a visible or external manner.
3. Describe some of the "flaws" in the world of nature which surround us.
4. Compare the sacraments and the sacramentals.
5. Each day we normally make use of some sacramental words or actions. Reflect on one or a few which are a part of your regular life.
6. Have you ever had any object blessed by a priest? What?
7. Outline the seasons of the Church year.
8. What were the sacramental spaces or sacred places you have been in during the past few years?
9. Explain the fuller type of ritual we can expect for "blessings" in the future.
10. Faith, devotion, and a careful celebration of the rite is critical for both the sacraments and the sacramentals. Why are those especially important for the sacramentals?

10

Special Signs of Grace

Nearly ten years ago I had a wonderful opportunity to lecture for six weeks in southern Africa. The extended series included a week in what was then called Rhodesia, a week in the tiny, mountainous kingdom of Lesotho, and four weeks in the beautiful, but troubled nation of South Africa.

Each weekend in that last country we were free from our speaking responsibilities and took the occasion to visit different black townships, offering Mass with those people in their own languages, and talking with them about various topics.

During one of those discussions, the Catholic priest, an Irish missionary working alone in a huge township with several hundred thousand black residents, described the puberty rite for young males in that culture.

This is truly a "passage" ritual, a complex series of actions which mark the lad's departure from childhood and his official entrance into manhood. Those in the neighborhood of a suitable age are assembled together, removed from their homes, whisked away to a specially prepared temporary dwelling, covered with painted decorations and clothes, kept isolated from others, placed under the tutelage of wise, older leaders, given challenging tasks, eventually circumcised, and finally returned after a number of days to the community where all join in a festive celebration welcoming and honoring these new "men" into their midst.

Ancient Sacred Signs

That puberty rite obviously has an ancient history, and its diverse rituals have evidently been handed down by word of mouth from generation to generation. Moreover, this rite and these rituals are clearly signs and symbols which point to something else and possess a unique, mysterious power to touch participants and observers. While not specifically Christian (my missionary host would like to integrate Catholic concepts with this tribal custom), the ceremony carries with it true religious meaning and references. The above illustration from South Africa underscores the truth that people of every age and in every culture have used signs and symbols to communicate, especially employing them as a means of expressing spiritual or religious meanings and values.

These signs and symbols may be special, mysterious and sacred: places (temples or churches, mountains or rivers, shrines or cities); actions (praying or singing, eating or fasting, dancing or meditating, stylized rituals or spontaneous gestures); objects (pictures or statues, vestments or vessels, tools or writings, food or drink, manufactured or natural); or persons (priests or victims, kings or saints, shamans or virgins, gurus or prophets).

For example, Moslems make pilgrimages to Mecca. Buddhist monks kneel and chant. Jews eat only certain foods. Native American medicine men are revered and called upon at expected or needed times.[1]

The ritual signs or symbolic actions fall into certain categories which involve a particular element and bear a common meaning. Thus:

Ritual Element	Common Meaning
Water	Express values of life and purity
Initiation	Dramatize value of belonging and responsibility
Meals	Represent attitudes of acceptance and sharing
Sacrifices	Symbolize notions of dependence and thankfulness
Atonement	Affirm the value of forgiving and being forgiven
Healing	Embody values of hope and health
Funeral	Express attitudes toward death
Marriage	Incorporate viewpoints about the sexes and the family
Ordination	Supports the value of centering one's life around sacred meaning and assures the continuing of sacred ritual in society[2]

These sacred actions have real meaning for those who participate in them, both for the central persons involved (the boys in that
South African puberty rite) and for those who support or, as it were,
surround the pivotal characters (the boys' families, wise instructors, and welcoming community). Moreover, repeated participation in them over the years brings back and deepens their meaning
for all concerned. Nevertheless, while meaningful, they always remain to an extent mysterious. People can never fully comprehend
or understand them.

The Jewish people or Israelites had their special sacred signs or
symbols. For them God spoke in a unique way through actual persons and events and through the written or spoken, handed down
record of those people or actions. Moreover, Judaism included both
temple rituals (offerings or sacrifices) and home rites (purifications
or symbolic meals).

Furthermore, when Jesus entered this world, he did so as a Jew,
but also as a person living in an atmosphere dominated by the Greek
and Roman culture. Both of these had their own sacred rituals and
signs.

All of this background information leads us to understand that
when Christ instituted seven special potent signs to help followers
walk faithfully in his footsteps, he was not so much creating totally new rituals as giving fresh, richer and additional meaning to
rites for the most part already existing. This short historical sketch
also makes three points about the seven Catholic sacraments:
(1) they correspond closely to the religious experiences of diverse
cultures and ages; (2) they reflect meanings important to other
religions; (3) they deal with human concerns common to all people. [3]

These points need to be kept in mind as we reflect upon the
explanation of the sacraments in preceding chapters. The truth of
those generalized assertions will likewise become clearer and more
evident if we re-examine each of those sacramental rituals in detail.

The Meaning of Sacrament

It is now time to look at the word "sacrament" itself. Where did
it originate? What does the term mean? How is it used today?

The dictionary tells us that "sacrament" comes from the Latin
word *sacramentum* whose root means to consecrate. Its definitions
of sacrament include: "A religious act, ceremony or practice that
is considered especially sacred as a sign or symbol of a deeper reality;" "a spiritual sign, seal or bond." [4]

That second definition takes us back to pre-Christian times when a *sacramentum* was a bond, seal, or sign in the form of a pledge of money or property. Parties to a lawsuit or contract deposited in a religious temple the pledge which would be forfeited by the one losing the suit or violating the contract. Later it came to mean an oath of allegiance made by soldiers to their commander and the gods of Rome. In both cases the sacrament involved a certain type of religious ceremony taking place in some kind of a sacred location.[5]

During the second century Christians adopted the term and used it for explaining the ceremony of Christian initiation to their Roman contemporaries. The three rites involved (baptism, confirmation, and Eucharist) were described as roughly parallel to the sacrament given to new soldiers. They signified in a ritual way that these new members of the Christian community had made an oath, pledge, or bond to remain faithful disciples of Christ and to give themselves in service to God.

Over the next few centuries the word "sacrament" came to be applied by Christians in a wider sense, covering any sacred symbol or ceremony. This included both Christian initiation and almost any blessing, liturgical feast, or holy object.[6]

St. Augustine during the fifth century defined a sacrament in very general terms as a "visible sign of an invisible reality" or "a visible sign of invisible grace." Moreover, he extended the notion of sacrament to encompass almost everything in the world, since according to him all of creation is a sign of God.[7]

Another word closely connected with sacrament was also used extensively in those early days among Christians. They employed the Latin term *mysterium* and spoke sometimes of their rituals as a mystery or mysteries. This conveyed the notion of a hidden, mysterious, sacred, incomprehensible reality or realities behind or beyond the visible sacramental actions.

Eventually "sacrament" for the most part denoted Christian rituals and mystery referred to the mysteries or teachings of the Christian faith.[8]

The Seven Sacraments

From the sixth to the eleventh century sacred rituals in the Church flourished and died, shifted in this direction or that, took one form or another—all in the face of a culture which made the strengthening, spread, or even survival of Christianity difficult.

The liturgical practices of that period, however, began to center around seven major rituals: the baptism of infants and converts, the confirmation of baptism by the bishop, the rite of penitence and forgiveness, the anointing of the dying, the ordaining of priests, the uniting of people in marriage, and the Eucharistic liturgy or Mass. There were many other sacred rites, but these came to be in practice the primary liturgical sacraments of the Church.[9]

Theologian Peter Lombard took that actual practice of the Church and gave it a theoretical basis. He developed a definition of these seven rites which made it possible to distinguish them from other sacred signs or ceremonies. In his *Sentences*, he wrote: "Something is properly called a sacrament because it is a sign of God's grace, and is such an image of invisible grace that it bears its likeness and exists as its cause."[10]

Other theologians and preachers accepted his analysis and by the end of the thirteenth century official synods or councils began to speak about *the* seven sacraments of the Catholic Church. The Second Council of Lyons in 1274, the Council of Florence in 1439, and the Council of Trent in 1547 all taught in this fashion."[11] The last convocation, reacting to Protestant developments which reduced the number of sacraments to two (baptism and Communion), sometimes only one, declared that "there are no more and no fewer than seven sacraments, namely, Baptism, Confirmation, Eucharist, Penance, Extreme Unction, Holy Orders and Matrimony."[12]

From the thirteenth century onward, therefore, while there were many additional sacred rites or actions in the Church which as signs and symbols pointed to other spiritual realities, normally the word "sacrament" applied only to these seven special signs of grace.

At the Second Vatican Council the bishops issued on December 4, 1963, the Constitution on the Sacred Liturgy. Its chapter on the sacraments simply presumes there are seven and describes their purpose from a pastoral point of view:

> They not only presuppose faith, but by words and objects they also nourish, strengthen, and express it. That is why they are called "sacraments of faith." They do, indeed, confer grace, but, in addition, the very act of celebrating them most effectively disposes the faithful to receive this grace to their profit, to worship God duly, and to practice charity.

> It is, therefore, of the greatest importance that the faithful should easily understand the sacramental signs, and should eagerly frequent those sacraments which were instituted to nourish the Christian life.[13]

The Sacraments Today

Our final and perhaps most important consideration deals with the nature of a sacrament in our world today. How do we identify a sacrament? What are its effects?

It will neither be easy nor possible to answer such questions in a totally satisfying manner. That is so because we are examining in this study divine mysteries, essentially incomprehensible realities, and sacred symbols which can only partially be understood or grasped.

Young people who studied religion in pre-Vatican II days probably memorized this simple and succinct definition of a sacrament: "It is an outward sign instituted by Christ designed to give grace." However, the following analysis of all three elements in that clear, terse formula will still leave us standing back in awe and with unanswered inquiries before our minds.

An Outward Sign

The first chapter described at some length the nature of signs and symbols. By their very definition, particularly in the case of symbols, they possess an elusive quality about them. Symbols trigger conscious and unconscious reactions within us, often without our knowing it or understanding why.

The seven sacraments are signs and, more, symbols as we described them. The bread, wine, and water with the words pronounced at a Eucharistic celebration, to illustrate, point to something beyond an ordinary meal. Moreover, those essential elements plus all the surrounding words, actions, and objects employed are likewise symbolic and impact us in all the ways we noted throughout chapter 1.

In addition there have been over the centuries and will be in the future regular changes in the way the Church celebrates each sacrament. For example, in this country priests prior to 1950 baptized babies generally in an area separated from the church proper and followed a Latin ritual. The mother normally was absent or, if present, stood only as an on-looker since the godmother held the infant. Today, the same priest might well perform the ceremony in the sanctuary before the Sunday congregation or community, follow a totally revised rite in English and arrange for the mother to hold the child.

At the Second Vatican Council the bishops established a general principle for the reform of the liturgical books which explained why there will be such future changes in our worship rites:

> In order that the Christian people may more certainly derive an abundance of graces from the sacred liturgy, holy Mother Church desires to undertake with great care a general restoration on the liturgy itself. For the liturgy is made up of unchangeable elements divinely instituted, and of elements subject to change. These latter not only may be changed but ought to be changed with the passage of time, if they have suffered from the intrusion of anything out of harmony with the inner nature of the liturgy or have become less suitable. In this restoration both texts and rites should be drawn up so as to express more clearly the holy things which they signify. The Christian people, as far as is possible, should be able to understand them with ease and take part in them fully, actively, and as a community. [14]

The Fathers of Vatican II reiterated the concept that with the passage of time certain features had crept into our sacramental rites rendering "their nature and purpose far from clear to the people of today. Hence some changes are necessary to adapt them to present-day needs." [15] The balance of that chapter in the Constitution on the Sacred Liturgy treats of specific reforms for each of the sacraments and sacramentals. Those have been completed now and consequently the manner in which we celebrate these rites today is quite different from the way we did so two decades ago.

But even when the basic sign employed is the same, shifts in the meaning of that element over the centuries alter our understanding of the particular sacrament. Thus, oil in the Middle East around the time of Christ was used as a salve and a medicine and consequently meant, in a ritual, health and healing; it was used to moisten dry skin and hair and thus meant leisure and luxury; it was used to anoint priests and kings, and therefore meant divine presence and power. Some of oil's uses and meanings continue in our time, but others no longer seem relevant or understandable. [16]

In a word, the very nature of a symbol, the changes in our sacramental rites, and the shift in meaning of the basic elements or ingredients contribute to make our grasp of the outward sign elusive and incomplete.

Instituted by Christ

The catechism definition held that the seven sacraments were instituted by the Lord Jesus. The question, however, is how and in what way?

Quite obviously Christ did not personally give to the twelve apostles and other disciples the exact details for celebrating baptism, the Eucharist, marriage, anointing of the sick, or the other sacraments. Most of the ritual gestures which surround each sacrament were instead developed by the Church over the years with rather constant additions and subtractions in the process.

Even seeking to find explicit references to all the sacraments in Scripture stretches a person's intellectual and imaginative efforts. Jesus, of course, did speak about baptism and the special meal of bread and wine to be repeated in his memory. But exactly linking his recorded words and the seven Catholic sacraments is somewhat difficult.

We have seen that the precise numbering of the sacraments as seven came later in the history of the Church. The Council of Trent (1545–1563) found references in the New Testament to all the sacraments, but it could not find an explicit record of Christ having instituted each of them. Moreover, contemporary Scripture scholars and Church historians in the light of studies today find the traditional connection between some of those biblical references and the sacraments subject for debate. [17]

The current explanation of the phrase "instituted by Christ" would maintain that Jesus came to preach the Gospel and build the Kingdom of God, that he established his Church as *the* sacrament manifesting God's Presence in the world, and that he gave this Church the guidance and power to develop in time seven sacraments as unique signs of grace for building the desired Kingdom.

Fr. William Bausch, a visionary pastor and popular writer on this subject, summarizes that approach:

> What we want to understand is that the seven sacraments were not handed down as-is personally from Jesus himself. They have a derivation from and association with the so-called Jewish sacraments, they are to be found in spirit in the scripture, but their exact numbering and defining were to be left to the church of a later, more analytical age. This will help us when we come to look at the revision of the rites in our time and explain how the sacraments could be revised to begin with. The answer, we now see, is that from the beginning the church has always had charge of the style and approaches to the essential "mysteries" of salvation left by Jesus. [18]

Historian Joseph Martos phrases the same notions:

> Catechisms used to say that the sacraments were instituted by Christ, and Catholic theologians still acknowledge a sense in which this is true. Historically speaking, however, we have to say that there is

no direct evidence that Jesus of Nazareth left his companions with a well-defined and complete set of sacramental rituals such as those that later developed in the church. On the other hand, there is ample evidence that the earliest followers of Jesus performed sacramental rituals which they believed were "from the Lord" or otherwise approved by God. They shared a special meal and prayed together, they baptized new believers and imposed hands on them, they anointed the sick and appointed leaders of the community. [19]

During the Middle Ages theologians analyzed the seven sacraments under the light of Greek philosophy with a Christian interpretation. These scholars sought to determine what was the "essence" or essential element of each sacrament in contrast to its "accidents" or non-essential elements. In addition, reflecting the Greek philosophical concepts of the day, they also tried to discover what was the "matter" and the "form" for all the sacraments.

The "matter" would be the sensible gestures or actions which could be seen, heard, touched, tasted, and smelt. The "form" was the meaning that these rituals possessed, a meaning often communicated through the words which accompanied those gestures or actions.

For example, lighting the candle or reading scriptural passages would be accidental dimensions of a baptism; the pouring of water and recitation of a formula would be essential elements of the sacrament. Moreover, the pouring of water over the candidate would be the proper matter for baptism; the words "I baptize you . . . ." would be the form which gives meaning to that action.

While those scholastic terms are not so universally accepted today, they still provide a clear, easy, and succinct albeit limited way of examining the sacraments. They have been used throughout this book to help explain each sacrament.

However we understand the "essence" of each sacrament as instituted by Christ, it would seem obvious that the "accidents" of every one have been developed by the Church, not directly by Jesus.

Designed to Give Grace

If it is difficult to grasp fully the meaning of the sacrament as an outward sign and impossible to understand completely how Christ instituted the seven sacraments, it is even more difficult and more impossible to capture totally the proper significance of that phrase "to give grace." We are in fact dealing here with a mystery of our faith.

Looking up the word "grace" in a secular dictionary provides us with a good indication of the term's complex and profound nature.

A copy of *Webster's Third New International Unabridged Dictionary* rests on a cabinet next to my desk. This absolutely massive text gives an entire column on one of its large pages over to the various definitions and explanations of "grace," far more space than most words receive.

It originates from a Latin root meaning "charm, favor, thanks" or "pleasing, beloved, grateful."

The first definition includes these alternatives:

> A beneficence or generosity shown by God to man . . . especially, divine favor unmerited by man.
>
> A free gift of God to man for his regeneration or sanctification: an influence emanating from God and acting for the spiritual well-being of the recipient.
>
> A state of acceptance with or of being pleasing to God: enjoyment of divine favor.
>
> A virtue or moral excellence regarded as coming from God. [20]

How do the sacraments confer, give, or bring about this grace? In what way are they signs of such grace? Is there one explanation of the manner in which they work?

Theologians have been struggling with these questions for centuries and have developed as many diverse approaches as there are dictionary definitions of grace. They know from experience that the sacraments produce definite results. Something actually happens. The baptized person becomes a member of the Church, the absolved individual walks away forgiven, the ordained begins to function in a special role, and the anointed enjoys a return to health or at least inner calmness.

The various theological analyses of these spiritual experiences or happenings are helpful, but can never exhaust the meaning of a sacrament. Nor does any one theological approach perfectly explain the sacramental phenomenon. Taken together, nevertheless, they provide us with a wider picture and better understanding of these seven special signs of grace.

Causes of Grace.

The sacraments have a certain God-given power within themselves to confer upon properly disposed recipients what is called sanctifying grace. Sanctifying grace refers to the gift of divine life conveyed to believers which makes people morally good and able to lead holy lives. Through this grace the risen Lord either begins to dwell within the person in a special way, restores to the individual an awareness of Christ's Presence that may have been lost through sin or deepens his presence within one who already possesses that gift.

Moreover, the sacraments also confer a supernatural stengthening usually called actual grace which enables the recipient to live out the responsibilities of the specific sacrament. For example, the actual grace connected with matrimony will strengthen spouses when faced with marital challenges and the actual grace linked with holy orders will enable bishops, priests, and deacons to discharge their ministerial functions in appropriate ways.

Three of the sacraments, baptism, confirmation and holy orders, likewise confer a lasting sacramental character or supernatural effect that makes one permanently a member of the Church, a confirmed Christian or a priest (deacon or bishop). These, therefore, cannot be repeated.

The sacramental rituals themselves, not the minister who performs them, are the channels through which the effects are received. Consequently, the personal holiness of the minister, while desirable, is not essential for the sacrament to have validity or impact. For example, a priest may be enslaved personally through human weakness by a destructive addiction that is even known in the community. Nevertheless, if he performs the proper ritual with a suitable intention, that Mass, baptism or reconciliation, to illustrate, would be valid, communicate grace and have spiritual power despite his scandalous behavior. The rite works regardless, although surely much less effectively.

Similarly, the sacrament achieves its results as long as the recipient possesses at least a fundamental openness and minimal awareness, although to receive its full influence the recipient needs to be more positively prepared and actively engaged in the rite.[21]

Signs of Faith.

The characteristics described in that last paragraph have led to some unfortunate false attitudes in the past and raised difficulties for theologians of the present.

The fact that the sacraments have power within themselves regardless of the minister's holiness or the recipient's devotion is a great pastoral blessing.

As a priest I have more than once been most grateful that the sacramental actions I was performing had a power beyond my limited human efforts to make them attractive. I also remember from my own experience, for example in receiving reconciliation or "going to confession," that it was comforting and encouraging to know that the Lord was working through this ritual despite the fact that the priest confessor's words or actions left something to be desired.

Nevertheless, the fact that the sacraments are causes of grace is also a pastoral challenge. The danger of that awareness and the difficulty raised by modern leaders of the Church centers around a certain magical approach to the sacraments which developed over the years.

The priest tended to concentrate on the essential words and actions alone, minimized his own faith or liturgical presence, and considered the people's active participation in the rite of insignificant importance. Recipients also fell into that trap of minimalism. As long as the baby had the water poured over its head, or a sinner heard the words of absolution, or the dying patient received the priest's anointing, nothing else mattered. Preparing for the ritual moment, celebrating it with faith, participating prayerfully in the ceremony and living out its consequences, seemed not crucial issues.

Without denying the "causes of grace" dimension in the sacraments, the Church, seeking to counteract such a near magical attitude, both during and subsequent to the Vatican Council also reminded us that these actions are "signs of faith."

In the words of the Constitution on the Sacred Liturgy, the sacraments:

> because they are signs . . . also instruct. They not only presuppose faith, but by words and objects they also nourish, strengthen, and express it. That is why they are called 'sacraments of faith.' They do, indeed, confer grace, but, in addition, the very act of celebrating them most effectively disposes the faithful to receive this grace to their profit, to worship God duly, and to practice charity.
>
> It is, therefore, of the greatest importance that the faithful should easily understand the sacramental signs, and should eagerly frequent those sacraments which were instituted to nourish the Christian life.[22]

The American bishops in a subsequent 1972 document on *Music in Catholic Worship* conveyed a similar message. According to this instruction, the sacraments as liturgical celebrations are not only causes of grace, but simultaneously signs of faith.

> To celebrate the liturgy means to do the action or perform the sign in such a way that its full meaning and impact shine forth in clear

and compelling fashion. Since liturgical signs are vehicles of communication and instruments of faith, they must be simple and comprehensible. Since they are directed to fellow human beings, they must be humanly attractive. They must be meaningful and appealing to the body of worshippers or they will fail to stir up faith and people will fail to worship the Father.[23]

Such a concept places a much greater responsibility upon the individual who ministers the sacrament, the person who receives it, and the people present who participate in the ritual celebration.

Acts of Christ

In the 1950s and 1960s a Dutch theologian named Edward Schillebeeckx took the philosophy of contemporary existentialism and integrated that with the Church's traditional understanding of the sacraments. According to this view, Christ is *the* sacrament, since Jesus most perfectly serves as a visible sign, points to, and reveals the invisible God to us. Our Lord did this during his life on earth and through his appearances after the Resurrection. However, Christ continues to be present today through his Church, which is likewise *the* sacrament of Jesus in the world today. The Church makes the divine mystery of God and Christ present to the world primarily in seven ways corresponding to the seven ways that Christ himself was a sacrament of God to others.

When we receive a sacrament, we undergo an existential encounter with the Lord. Christ is present, acts through the sacramental ritual, and we in turn meet the risen Lord there and encounter him. As in all deeply personal encounters we do or at least should discover something of the mystery of who Jesus is through that experience. It reveals a transcendent, divine reality or person to us and opens up the possibility that we may fall in love with God through Christ.[24]

Vatican Council Fathers supported such a concept when in a famous paragraph of the Constitution on the Sacred Liturgy they spoke of the many presences of Christ in the Church and especially in its liturgical celebrations:

> Christ is always present in his Church, especially in her liturgical celebrations. He is present in the Sacrifice of the Mass not only in the person of his minister, "the same now offering, through the ministry of priests, who formerly offered himself on the cross," but especially in the eucharistic species. By his power he is present in the sacraments so that when anybody baptizes it is really Christ himself

who baptizes. He is present in his word since it is he himself who speaks when the holy scriptures are read in the Church. Lastly, he is present when the Church prays and sings, for he has promised "where two or three are gathered together in my name there am I in the midst of them" (Matt 18:20).[25]

It truly is then Christ who baptizes, confirms, marries, ordains, forgives, and anoints the recipient. The person receiving the sacrament is actively meeting the risen Jesus in faith, encountering the Savior through special, visible words, objects, and actions.

Symbols of the Church.

This description or characteristic of the sacraments flows from the previous notion that they are acts of Christ. The Church, as we noted, is the risen Lord present in this world today as he has been since its beginning on Pentecost and will continue until the end of the ages. Christ instituted the Church to carry on his work of bringing people into an existential contact with the Father. This flesh and blood, here and now, visible and active Church is therefore called by some theologians the fundamental sacrament or foundational reality.

The European Jesuit theologian Karl Rahner, in parallel fashion to his contemporary Schillebeeckx, sought to connect the modern philosophical approach of phenomenology to the Roman Catholic traditional notion of the sacraments.[26] According to this philosophy of human life, we reveal our inner selves to one another by physical gestures and our bodily presence. Thus these elements have a symbolic nature to them: they both disclose who we are to one another, but simultaneously enhance our understanding of each other.

So, too, in the sacraments, those acts of the Church, we as members express who we are to God and at the same time we learn and grow through those ritual actions in our awareness of who God is and what God is doing for and in us. We recognize that God in Christ summons us to self-transcendence, to become more than we are after the example and through the power of Jesus, God's son.

In Rahner's words, "The sacraments make concrete and actual, for the life of the individual, the symbolic reality of the Church as the primary sacrament and therefore constitute at once, in keeping with the nature of the Church, a symbolic reality."[27]

The Constitution on the Sacred Liturgy tells us that the liturgy, including and especially the sacraments, is the "full public worship . . . performed by the Mystical Body of Jesus Christ [the Church], that is, by the Head and his Members."[28] Liturgical celebrations, the document continues, are not private functions but are celebrations of the Church. They "pertain to the whole Body of the Church. They manifest it, and have effects upon it."[29] As a practical consequence of that theology, the Vatican decree emphasizes that the offering of the Mass and the administration of the sacraments are meant to be celebrated in common with the faithful present and actively participating rather than in an individual and quasi-private way.[30]

All of this may seem extremely theoretical, heavy reading and perhaps hard to grasp. It has, however, extremely practical consequences. Such an awareness of the sacraments leads, for example, to the practice of baptizing infants within the context of Sunday Mass as a fuller sign of the children being welcomed into the Church. It also means that when a sick person is anointed by the priest, the entire Church here and abroad, those living and those who have gone beyond, are praying with and through the priest at the bedside of the ailing individual.

Helps for Life's Major Moments.

A crisis is a turning point in one's life. We usually employ the term when the situation involves a major matter and a poor choice may result in some serious disaster. However, there are countless, even daily crisis moments in each person's life, occasions when we make decisions to go here rather than there, move in this direction rather than in that one. When the issues at stake are particularly significant, we label the crisis time a major moment.

Familiar natural crises touch our existence frequently in one way or another: birth, growth, guilt, forgiveness, maturity, love, sickness, death, and bereavement. But we likewise experience personal, community, national, and worldwide major moments: divorce after years of marriage or job promotion requiring transfer, a local hideous murder or high school athletic championship, a national election or Thanksgiving Day observance, hunger in Africa, or the Olympic Games.

In all of these we possess a human need to make sense out of the reality which we experience, give it meaning, learn what to do about it, find strength to cope with the burdens, and discover ways to express joy over the blessings. Those are teachable and touchable moments. We are open to an experience of God in these contexts and seek to situate the divine in the midst of them. The sacramental rituals are incredibly rich in their ability to accomplish this, to transform the meaning of these human experiences.

The American theologian Bernard Cooke has written and taught extensively along this line. For him the sacraments bring the life, death and resurrection of Jesus into the nitty-gritty of our human lives which gives those experiences meaning and offers a new look at life leading to happiness and fulfillment.[31] He writes:

> Baptism means dying to other interpretations of life and rising to a life charged with redemptive meaning. Confirmation marks a continuation of the new life begun in baptism. Reconciliation means accepting forgiveness from God and offering it to others. Anointing reinterprets the meaning of sickness for those who are suffering and makes death alive with possibilities. Marriage reveals the meaning of Christ's fidelity to his church. Ordination changes the meaning of service from servitude to ministry. In the eucharistic liturgy Christians discover the meaning of resurrected living for their daily experiences, and celebrate that continually rediscovered meaning.[32]

The sacraments, therefore, give wisdom and power, insight and inspiration, guidance and strength to help us through life's journey and especially to assist us during its major moments.

Central to the Process of Our Growth.

Certain current philosophers, most notably Alfred North Whitehead, see life as basically continuous becoming. When we reflect on our experiences, we conclude that our lives far from being static or unchanging are always flowing, changing, and dynamic. For these thinkers, process is a primary reality which affects all beings or entities and lasts through time.[33] In that context we are both the sum of our total past experiences, and at the same time we now envisage future possibilities which shape the direction of our personal development.

God is very much part of this past, present, and future process. God is calling us to become more than we were before or are now: God calls us to transcendence. According to that outlook, "God is thus present in every act of becoming, suggesting the ways that it may become its best self and even go beyond itself, taking into consideration what it has already become and the environment through which it will progress, both of which impose limitations on its becoming."[34]

The sacraments in a special way bring this power or causality of God into human lives. They recall how Jesus once perfectly realized the potential before him and now summons us to walk in similar total fidelity to God's call. They not only bring back to mind what Christ did in the past, they also make him present now for us. Through that here and now Presence, Jesus likewise opens up possibilities for the future. The sacraments therefore in effect realize Christ's energizing presence in our todays and tomorrows.

Someone once said, "When we stop growing, we start dying." Following Christ means repeated changes of heart and constant new beginnings. We are pilgrims in process, seeking the Father's will and a kingdom yet to come. The sacraments uniquely accompany us on that constant, on-going journey or process forward.

Calls to Conversion.

In the last quarter of a century, the charismatic renewal has mushroomed rapidly both in this country and beyond. Its external characteristics have become somewhat familiar to most Roman Catholics whether they like or dislike, approve or disapprove of them: praying or singing in tongues, spontaneous prayer expressed in word and gesture, regular use of the Bible, laying on of hands, prayer for healing, and frequent mention of baptism in the Spirit.

Reflective leaders, however, see the essential element of the charismatic renewal as "conversion." The conversion here means not necessarily changing from one or no religion to Catholicism, but instead a total conversion or change of a person's entire life. This entails accepting Christ as one's personal savior and subsequently altering the way we feel and behave, think, and make decisions. The Spirit active in this process leads us to trust God and to discover the Lord's revelation in Scripture, calls us to repentance, softens our stubbornness, affects our behavior, moves us to act without self-interest, prompts us creatively to change the world, and urges us to share what we possess with others. [35]

While the release of the Spirit and the outpouring of God's grace often come outside the seven sacramental rites, Catholic charismatics nevertheless generally do recognize the power of God in those rituals and consider them as signs of God's desire and pledge to deepen a relationship with us. These holy signs promise the gifts of grace believers seek: "healing, nourishing, cleansing, freeing, consecrating, blessing, empowering us to accept his reign in our lives and deepening our covenant with him and his people." [36] Accord-

ing to this viewpoint, the sacraments, to be effective, demand a
personal commitment of faith, a total engagement of ourself and
a change of heart which will eventually transform our lives.

Instruments of Liberation.

In South America the concerns of poverty and oppression have
brought thinkers, led by the Jesuit Juan Luis Segundo, to examine
the sacraments in terms of liberation theology and thus to see how
they can transform the Church and reform society.[37] The emphasis,
then, is on the social impact of the rites rather than on their
influence upon a person's individual relationship to God.

Without denying the need for the sacraments or the power of
grace, Segundo teaches that we must interpret the rites in terms
of this world rather than the next. For him the Church "is the community of those who are doing God's will, making Christ present
in the world and making grace alive in history through their concern for others."[38] That concern for others prompts people to aid
those who struggle to liberate themselves from various forces which
hold them enslaved.

More specifically in terms of a sacrament, Segundo stresses:

> On the occasion of each sacrament it should present the Christian
> people with their present, concrete, existential situation. It should
> pose this situation as a problem that challenges them and calls for
> their response. And it should also show divine revelation to be an
> element capable of helping them to face up to this challenge.[39]

Conclusion

The sacraments have been designed by Christ as outward signs
"to give grace." We have sought to explain this last phrase by noting that the seven rites are causes of grace, signs of faith, acts of
Christ, symbols of the Church, helps for life's major moments, central to the process of growth, calls to conversion, and instruments
of liberation.

None of these phrases exhausts the meaning of the sacraments.
On the other hand, if we have omitted one approach, our understanding of the sacraments is inadequate. At the same time, if we
exaggerate a particular concept, our view of the sacraments becomes
distorted. However, when we examine all of these explanations or
phrases together, our picture of what the sacraments really are becomes better, clearer, and fuller.

Nevertheless, it is good to recall often that these seven special signs of grace are mysteries. Thus, never in our human condition can we totally comprehend the depth, the meaning and the power of the Catholic sacraments.

Discussion Questions

1. Are you familiar through experience, reading, study, or conversation with the religious rituals of others who are neither Catholic nor Christian, for example, Jewish people, Moslems, or early Native Americans? Describe that rite or those rites.

2. Explain the notion of "sacrament" as a pledge and its understanding by early Christians; also explain the concept of "mystery" as understood by the first followers of Christ.

3. When did the Church finally specify the precise number of sacraments?

4. Talk with some older people who remember baptisms or marriages thirty or forty years ago and some who have celebrated those sacraments recently. What were the differences? What was identical? By what authority did the Church change the outward sign or the rituals of these sacraments? Why did the Church do so?

5. How do most Church leaders today explain the teaching that "the sacraments were instituted by Christ"?

6. The sacraments are both causes of grace and signs of faith. Remembering that they are causes of grace can prove very helpful to us at times; forgetting that they must also be signs of faith can at the same moment prove detrimental to our spiritual growth. Give illustrations which explain the potential benefit and danger of both approaches.

7. What are the various ways through which Christ is present and we meet him in our liturgical celebrations?

8. Give two examples which underscore the truth that the sacraments are symbols or actions of the Church.

9. Identify some major moments in peoples lives and describe how the sacraments provided help on those occasions.

10. Why is no one explanation of the sacraments adequate? Can we ever fully grasp their meaning? How then should we deal with theological approaches to the sacraments, particularly those diverse attempts to explain the fact that the sacraments have been designed to give grace?

Resource Reading

General Texts on the Sacraments

The following books, or substantial parts of them, treat the sacraments in general, all of the sacraments, or at least several of the sacraments:

Bausch, William J. *A New Look at the Sacraments.* West Mystic, Conn.: Twenty-Third Publications, 1977.

Flannery, Austin, ed. "Constitution on the Sacred Liturgy," *Vatican Council II: The Conciliar and Post Conciliar Documents*, vol. 1. Collegeville: The Liturgical Press, 1975.

Martos, Joseph. *Doors to the Sacred.* New York: Doubleday and Company, Inc., 1981.

_____. *The Catholic Sacraments.* Wilmington: Michael Glazier, Inc., 1983.

McBrien, Richard P. *Catholicism.* Minneapolis: Winston Press, 1981, 731–816.

The Rites vols. I and II. New York: Pueblo Publishing Co., 1976, 1980.

Roguet, A.M. *Christ Acts Through Sacraments.* Collegeville, The Liturgical Press, 1961.

Specific Texts for Each Chapter

The following books or sections of them treat more specifically each sacrament or the topic of that particular chapter:

Chapter 1   More Than Meets the Eye

Champlin, Joseph M. *The Proper Balance.* Notre Dame, Ind.: Ave Maria Press, 1981. 53–58.

Collins, Patrick W. *More Than Meets the Eye.* New York: Paulist Press, 1983, chapter 3.

Dulles, Avery. *Models of the Church.* Garden City, N.Y.: Doubleday and Company, Inc., 1974, 17–20.

Guzie, Tad. *The Book of Sacramental Basics.* New York: Paulist Press, 1981, chapter 3.

Chapter 2   Baptism: A New Life and a New Family

Marsh, Thomas A. *Gift of Community*. Wilmington: Michael Glazier, Inc., 1984.

Chapter 3   Confirmation: Gift of the Spirit

Marsh, Thomas A. *Gift of Community*. Wilmington: Michael Glazier, Inc., 1984.

Chapter 4   The Eucharist: Worship, Food, and Presence

Champlin, Joseph M. *An Important Office of Immense Love*. New York: Paulist Press, 1980, 1984.
Duffy, Regis. *Real Presence*. San Francisco: Harper and Row, 1982.
Keifer, Ralph A. *Blessed and Broken*. Wilmington: Michael Glazier, Inc., 1982.
Liturgy Documentary Series #2, "General Instruction of the Roman Missal." Washington: United States Catholic Conference Publishing Services, 1982.
Mick, Lawrence E. *To Live As We Worship*. Collegeville: The Liturgical Press, 1984.

Chapter 5   Penance: Forgiveness and Growth

Champlin, Joseph M. *Together in Peace: Penitent's, Priest's and Children's Editions*. Notre Dame, Ind: Ave Maria Press, 1975, 1976.
_____. *Why Go to Confession?* Los Angeles: Franciscan Communications, 1982.
Hellwig, Monica. *Sign of Reconciliation and Conversion*. Wilmington: Michael Glazier, Inc., 1982.
John Paul II, Pope. *Reconciliation and Penance*. Washington: Office of Publishing and Promotion Services, United States Catholic Conference, 1984.
Origins, N C Documentary Service, Washington, vol. 13, nos. 19–22, 31, 1983–1984.

Chapter 6   Anointing: Healing, Courage, and Hope

Champlin, Joseph M. *Healing in the Catholic Church*. Huntington, Ind.: Our Sunday Visitor, Inc., 1985.
_____. *Through Death to Life*. Notre Dame, Ind.: Ave Maria Press, 1979.
_____. *Together by Your Side*. Notre Dame, Ind.: Ave Maria Press, 1979.
Empereur, James L. *Prophetic Anointing*. Wilmington: Michael Glazier, Inc., 1982.
Gusmer, Charles W. *And You Visited Me: Sacramental Ministry for the Sick and the Dying*. New York: Pueblo Publishing Co., 1984.
Pastoral Care of the Sick: Rites of Anointing and Viaticum, International Committee on English in the Liturgy. Collegeville: The Liturgical Press, 1983.

Chapter 7   Matrimony: Building the Little Church

Catoir, John T. *Catholics and Broken Marriage*. Notre Dame, Ind.: Ave Maria Press, 1979).
Champlin, Joseph M. *Together for Life*. Notre Dame, Ind.: Ave Maria Press, 1970.
_____. *Together for Life: A Marriage Preparation Course*. Allen, Tex: Argus Communications, 1985.
John Paul II, Pope. *On the Family*, Apostolic Exhortation of December 15, 1981. Washington: Office of Publishing Services, United States Catholic Conference, 1982.

Kelly, Kevin T. *Divorce and Second Marriage.* New York: The Seabury Press, 1983.
Lawless, Richard M. *When Love Unites the Church.* St. Meinrad, Indiana: Abbey Press, 1982.
Thomas, David M. *Christian Marriage.* Wilmington: Michael Glazier, Inc., 1983.
Young, James J. *Ministering to the Divorced Catholic.* New York: Paulist Press, 1979.

Chapter 8   Holy Orders: Continuing the Larger Church

Bishop's Committee on the Liturgy. *The Deacon: Minister of Word and Sacrament: Study Text VI.* Washington: Publications Office, United States Catholic Conference, 1979.
Cunningham, Agnes. *The Role of Women in Ecclesial Ministry: Biblical and Patristic Foundations.* Washington: Publications Office, United States Catholic Conference, 1976.
John Paul II, Pope. "A Letter to Priests," April 9, 1979. Washington: "Origins," N C Documentary Service, vol. 8, no. 44, April 19, 1979.
Mitchell, Nathan. *Mission and Ministry.* Wilmington: Michael Glazier, Inc., 1982.

Chapter 9   Sacramentals: Connecting the Creator and Creation

Brett, Lawrence F. X. *Redeemed Creation: Sacramentals Today.* Wilmington: Michael Glazier, Inc., 1984.
Simons, Thomas G. *Blessings.* Saratoga, Calif.: Resource Publications, Inc., 1981.
_____. *Blessings for God's People.* Notre Dame, Ind.: Ave Maria Press, 1983.

Chapter 10   Seven Special Signs of Grace

Bishops' Committee on the Liturgy, National Conference of Catholic Bishops, *Music in Catholic Worship,* revised ed. Washington: United States Catholic Conference Publications Office, 1983, 9–13.
Ott, Ludwig. *Fundamentals of Catholic Dogma.* St. Louis: B. Herder Book Company, 1954, 323–47.

Notes

Chapter 1   *More Than Meets the Eye*

1. Joseph Martos, *The Catholic Sacraments* (Wilmington: Michael Glazier, Inc., 1983) 28–30.

2. Joseph M. Champlin, *The Proper Balance* (Notre Dame, Indiana: Ave Maria Press, 1981) 53–58.

3. Patrick W. Collins, *More Than Meets the Eye* (New York: Paulist Press, 1983) 49.

4. *Ibid.* 48–49.

5. Avery Dulles, *Models of the Church* (Garden City, N.Y.: Doubleday and Company, Inc., 1974) 20.

6. William J. Bausch, *A New Look at the Sacraments* (West Mystic, Conn.: Twenty-Third Publications, 1977) 6–7, 11–12.

7. Dulles, *Models of the Church* 18–20.

8. Richard P. McBrien, *Catholicism* (Minneapolis: Winston Press, 1981) 1182.

9. Darryl Ducote, "Look Beyond." From the F.E.L. Publications, Ltd., Recording, "Tell the World." Text and music © 1969.

Note: Throughout this book there are frequent quotations from liturgical books. The official translation of those texts at times contains sexist language. A revision to remove such exclusive terms is underway by the original translating committee, but has not yet been completed. Moreover, references to or excerpts from certain older books may include an occasional sexist term, and the integrity of that original text has been observed.

Chapter 2   *Baptism: A New Life and a New Family*

1. *The Rites* (New York: Pueblo Publishing Company, 1976) "Christian Initiation of Adults," articles 4–8, 27, pp. 20–22, 28.

2. *Ibid.* article 7, p. 21.

3. *Ibid.* "Baptism for Children," article 9, p. 191.

4. *Ibid.* article 2, p. 188.

5. *Ibid.* "Christian Initiation," articles 18–23, pp. 8–9.

6. Joseph Martos, *Doors to the Sacred* (Garden City, N.Y.: Doubleday and Company, 1981) 163–65.

7. *The Rites* articles 18–22, p. 8.

8. Acts 2:38; 8:16; 10:48; 19:5; 22:16.

9. Thomas A. Marsh, *Gift of Community* (Wilmington: Michael Glazier, Inc., 1984) 49–50.

10. A.M. Roguet, *Christ Acts Through Sacraments* (Collegeville: The Liturgical Press, 1961) 56–57.

11. *The Rites* articles 72–78, pp. 214–15.

12. *Ibid.* article 10, p. 6. See *Code of Canon Law*, canons 872–874. See also *Emendations in the Liturgical Books Following Upon the New Code of Canon Law* (Washington: International Commission on English in the Liturgy, 1984) 12–13.

13. *Ibid.* article 8, p. 6.

14. *Ibid.* articles 27, p. 9; 9–10, p. 191.

15. *Ibid.* article 79, p. 215.

16. *Ibid.* article 86, p. 218.

17. Roguet, *Christ Acts Through Sacraments* 51–52.

18. *The Rites* article 87, p. 218.

19. *Ibid.* article 98, p. 223.

20. *Ibid.* articles 89–96, pp. 220–22.

21. *Ibid.* articles 2, 4, pp. 188–89.

22. *Ibid.* article 3, p. 188.

23. *Ibid.* articles 4–8, pp. 188–91.

24. *Ibid.* article 8, p. 190.

25. *Ibid.* article 99, pp. 223–24.

26. *Ibid.* article 100, p. 224.

27. Marsh, *Gift of Community* 22–24.

28. See note 8.

29. Marsh, *Gift of Community* chapter 5, 68–101.

30. *Ibid.* 62–63.

31. *The Rites* articles 3–6, pp. 4–5.

32. *Ibid.* articles 1–2, pp. 3–4.

Chapter 3   *Confirmation: Gift of the Spirit*

1. *The Rites* (New York: Pueblo Publishing Company, 1976) 292.

2. *Ibid.* 303.

3. *Ibid.* 309.

4. *Ibid.* 292.

5. *Ibid.* article 9, p. 301.

6. *Ibid.* no. 25, p. 309.

7. *Ibid.* 296, 310.

8. *Ibid.* 295.

9. *Ibid.* articles 7–8, pp. 299–300. See *Emendations in the Liturgical Books Following Upon the New Code of Canon Law* 16.

10. *Ibid.* article 5, p. 299. See *Emendations in the Liturgical Books Following Upon the New Code of Canon Law* 15.

11. *Ibid.* article 6, p. 299.

12. *Ibid.* no. 26, p. 309.

13. *Ibid.* article 13, p. 303.

14. Joseph Martos, *Doors to the Sacred* (Garden City, N.Y.: Doubleday and Company, 1981) 205.

15. Thomas A. Marsh, *Gift of Community* (Wilmington: Michael Glazier, Inc., 1984) 59–61.

16. Martos, *Doors to the Sacred* 212.

17. Richard P. McBrien, *Catholicism* (Minneapolis: Winston Press, 1981) 754–57.

18. A. M. Roguet, *Christ Acts Through Sacraments* (Collegeville: The Liturgical Press, 1961) 65.

19. *The Rites* articles 1–2, p. 298.

20. *Ibid.* article 9, p. 301.

21. Gal 5:16-26; *The Rites* article 4, p. 299.

22. Joseph M. Champlin, *Behind Closed Doors* (New York: Paulist Press, 1984) 135–47.

23. *The Rites* article 5, p. 5.

Chapter 4   The Eucharist: Worship, Food, and Presence

1. *General Instruction of the Roman Missal.* (Washington: Office of Publishing Services, United States Catholic Conferences, 1982) articles 1, 7, 8, 48, 56; pp. 21, 23, 31, 33.

2. *Code of Canon Law* 897–898.

3. Joseph Martos, *Doors to the Sacred* (Garden City, N.Y.: Doubleday and Company, 1981) 239–43.

4. *Ibid.* 233–43.

5. *Ibid.* 243.

6. *Ibid.* 248.

7. *Ibid.* 263.

8. To summarize the long and complex history of the Mass in such a few pages is a difficult and risky task to say the least. My purpose here was merely to show the general trends and overall picture. There are ample books which give a thorough treatment of the eucharistic liturgy's history. *Doors to the Sacred*, chapter VIII, pp. 231–306 presents a good summary. The classic text is Josef Jungmann's massive volume *The Mass of the Roman Rite*, summarized and updated in The Liturgical Press's 1976 book by Jungmann, *The Mass.*

9. *General Instruction of the Roman Missal* article 7, p. 23.

10. *Ibid.* article 8, p. 23.

11. Joseph M. Champlin, *An Important Office of Immense Love* (New York: Paulist Press, 1984) 77–80. Two documents published by the U.S. Bishops' Committee on the Liturgy (Washington: U.S.C.C. Publications Office) present more details about the historical and legal dimensions of Communion in the Catholic Church: *The Body of Christ* (1977) and *This Holy and Living Sacrifice* (1985).

12. *Code of Canon Law* 913.

13. *Ibid.* 919.

14. *Ibid.* 916.

15. *Ibid.* 914.

16. *Ibid.* 920.

17. *Ibid.* 917.

18. St. Thomas Aquinas, *Summa Theologica (Westminster, Md.: Christian Classics, 1981) vol. V, III a, Q. 79, article 1, p. 2474.*

19. *The Rites,* "Holy Communion and Worship of the Eucharist Outside Mass" (New York: Pueblo Publishing Company, 1976) 453.

20. *Ibid.* article 6, p. 457.

21. *Ibid.* article 9, p. 457.

22. *Ibid.* article 11, p. 458.

23. *Ibid.* article 84, p. 486.

24. *Ibid.* article 85, p. 486.

25. *Ibid.* article 89, pp. 487–88.

26. *Ibid.* article 80, pp. 484–85.

Chapter 5   Penance: Forgiveness and Growth

1. Noah Gordon, *The Rabbi* (New York: Fawcett World Library, 1965) 178–79.

2. David K. O'Rourke, *A Process Called Conversion* (Garden City, N.Y.: Doubleday and Company, 1985) 23–32.

3. Pope John Paul II, *Reconciliation and Penance* (Washington: Office of Publishing and Promotion Services, United States Catholic Conference, December 2, 1984) 94.

4. O'Rourke, *A Process Called Conversion* 33.

5. Pope John Paul II, *Reconciliation and Penance* 29–30.

6. Richard P. McBrien, *Catholicism* (Minneapolis: Winston Press, 1981) 777

7. *The Rites* "Rite of Penance," (New York: Pueblo Publishing Company, 1976) 342.

8. *Ibid.* 342.

9. *The Rites* "Anointing and Pastoral Care of the Sick," 584.

10. *The Rites* "Rite of Penance," 342.

11. McBrien, *Catholicism* 778.

12. *Ibid.* 779.

13. *Ibid.* 778–79.

14. *Ibid.* 780.

15. *The Rites* "Rite of Penance," 339–40.

16. Pope John Paul II, *Reconciliation and Penance.*

17. Bishops' Committee on the Liturgy, *Study Text 4: Rite of Penance* (Washington: Publications Office, United States Catholic Conference, 1975) 23.

18. *The Code of Canon Law: A Text and Commentary*, Coriden, Green, and Heintschel, eds. (New York: Paulist Press, 1985) 681.

19. Joseph M. Champlin, *Together in Peace: Penitent's Edition* (Notre Dame Ind.: Ave Maria Press, 1974) 103. A priest's edition of this text contains the penitent's edition, the complete rite of penance and several other explanatory chapters. A children's edition adapts the adult penitent's edition to the mentality of elementary school age young people. Both the penitent's and children's editions include an abundance of scriptural texts, prayers, and comments designed to help the individual derive the maximum benefit from this reformed rite.

20. Joseph M. Champlin, *Why Go to Confession?* (Los Angeles: Franciscan Communications, 1982) 10–12. This booklet explains in a detailed question and answer format both why and how to go to confession as well as suggesting ways to make the sacrament effective for our lives.

21. *The Rites* "Rite of Penance," 365–75.

22. *Ibid.* article 22, p. 352.

23. *Ibid.* articles 31, 34, pp. 355–56.

24. See *Origins*, N C Documentary Service, Washington, vol. 13, nos. 19, 20, 21, 22, 31 for 1983–1984.

25. Pope John Paul II, *Reconciliation and Penance* 132.
26. Champlin, *Why Go to Confession?* 30.
27. Pope John Paul II, *Reconciliation and Penance* 130.
28. See footnotes 19–20 for help in this regard.
29. *The Rites* "Rite of Penance," article 7, pp. 346–47.

Chapter 6   Anointing: Healing, Courage, and Hope

1. Joseph M. Champlin, *Healing in the Catholic Church* (Huntington, Ind., 1985) 35. Many parts of this chapter are taken from or refer to this book, which deals in more complete fashion with various human ailments and how God did and does heal them.
2. *Ibid.* 61–62.
3. *Pastoral Care of the Sick: Rites of Anointing and Viaticum*, International Committee on English in the Liturgy (Collegeville: The Liturgical Press, 1983) 5.
4. Champlin, *Healing in the Catholic Church* 64–66. Two excellent contemporary studies of this sacrament contain good sections on the history of anointing and serve as foundations for the historical part of this chapter. James L. Empereur, *Prophetic Anointing* (Wilmington: Michael Glazier, Inc., 1982), Charles W. Gusmer, *And You Visited Me: Sacramental Ministry for the Sick and the Dying* (New York: Pueblo Publishing Co., 1984).
5. *Ibid.* 70–71.
6. *Pastoral Care of the Sick* article 42, p. 24.
7. *Ibid.* article 5, p. 12.
8. *Ibid.* article 6, p. 12.
9. *Ibid.* article 124, p. 94.
10. *Ibid.* article 125, pp. 95–96.
11. *Ibid.* article 130, p. 101.
12. *Ibid.* article 125, p. 95.
13. *Ibid.* article 8, p. 13.
14. *Ibid.* articles 9–15, pp. 13–14; article 102, p. 76; article 53, p. 27.
15. *Ibid.* p. 8, article 124, p. 94; article 107, p. 77.
16. *Ibid.* article 122, p. 91.
17. *Ibid.* article 121, p. 91.
18. *Ibid.* article 106, p. 77.
19. *Ibid.* article 7, p. 12.
20. *Ibid.* article 72, p. 50.
21. *Ibid.*
22. *Ibid.* article 73, p. 51.
23. *Ibid.* article 175, p. 136.
24. *Ibid.* article 161, p. 130.
25. *Ibid.* article 163, p. 131.
26. *Ibid.* article 177, p. 136.
27. *Ibid.* article 179, p. 137.
28. *Ibid.* article 180, p. 137.
29. *Ibid.* article 181, pp. 137–38.
30. *Ibid.* article 183, p. 138.
31. *Ibid.* article 212, p. 162.
32. *Ibid.* article 215, p. 163.

33. Joseph M. Champlin, *Together by Your Side* (Notre Dame, Ind.: Ave Maria Press, 1979). An audio-cassette kit from the same publisher and by the same name with the subtitle "A Program on How to Comfort the Sick, the Dying and the Bereaved" describes in detail with many examples and suggestions how the ministry to the sick can be carried out. It also provides a training suggestion for forming volunteers to serve the dying, bereaved, and grieving.

Chapter 7   Matrimony: Building the Little Church

1. William Barclay, *The Daily Study Bible Series*, "The Gospel of John" (Philadelphia: The Westminster Press, 1977) I, 95–99.

2. Joseph Martos, *Doors to the Sacred* (Garden City, N.Y. Doubleday and Company, 1981) 400–05.

3. David M. Thomas, *Christian Marriage* (Wilmington: Michael Glazier, Inc., 1983) 86.

4. Martos, *Doors to the Sacred* 405–06.

5. *Ibid.* 425.

6. *Ibid.* 428.

7. Richard P. McBrien, *Catholicism* (Minneapolis, Winston Press, 1981) 790.

8. Martos, *Doors to the Sacred* 431.

9. *Ibid.* 438.

10. *The Rites* (New York: Pueblo Publishing Company, 1976) "Rite of Marriage," 529–70.

11. Joseph M. Champlin, *Together for Life* (Notre Dame, Ind.: Ave Maria Press, 1970). The fact that this manual alone (there are others) for the couple to be used in preparing the ceremony has gone through over thirty printings and three million copies in the past fifteen years indicates how popular the revised ritual has been for both clergy and engaged.

12. *Code of Canon Law* Canons 1055–1057.

13. Champlin, *Together for Life* 73.

14. Austin Flannery, ed., *Vatican Council II: The Conciliar and Post Conciliar Documents*, vol. 1, (Collegeville: The Liturgical Press, 1975) "Decree on the Apostolate of Lay People," article 11.

15. Joseph M. Champlin, *Together for Life: A Marriage Preparation Course* (Allen, Texas: Argus Communications, 1985). This video cassette program with its companion resource booklet develops in detail these points about the covenant aspect of matrimony. Moreover, the "Introduction" to the *Rite of Marriage*, articles 1–7 on the "Importance and Dignity of the Sacrament of Matrimony" succinctly expresses some of these concepts (cf. Joseph M. Champlin, *Together for Life* 90).

16. Champlin, *Together for Life* 90, article 7.

17. *Code of Canon Law*, Canon 1063.

18. Flannery, *Vatican Council II: The Conciliar and Post Conciliar Documents* "Decree on the Apostolate of Lay People," vol. 1, article 11.

19. David M. Thomas, *Christian Marriage* 107. Cf. Pope John Paul II, *On the Family*, "Apostolic Exhortation of December 15, 1981" (Washington: Office of Publishing Services, United States Catholic Conference, 1982) article 68, pp. 65–67.

20. Richard M. Lawless, *When Love Unites the Church* (St. Meinrad, Ind.: Abbey Press, 1982).

21. Champlin, *Together for Life* 65, 91–94.

22. See *Ministering to the Divorced Catholic*. James J. Young, ed. (New York: Paulist Press, 1979) 25.

23. McBrien, *Catholicism* 794.

24. John T. Catoir, *Catholics and Broken Marriage* (Notre Dame, Ind.: Ave Maria Press, 1979) 34.

25. McBrien, *Catholicism* 796.

Chapter 8   Holy Orders: Continuing the Larger Church

1. Austin Flannery, ed., *Vatican Council II: The Conciliar and Post Conciliar Documents*, vol. 1 (Collegeville: The Liturgical Press, 1975) "Decree on the Training of Priests" (1965) 707–24; "Decree on the Ministry and Life of Priests" (1965) 863–902.

2. *The Rites* vol. 2 (New York: Pueblo Publishing Company, 1980) "Apostolic Letter Issued *Motu Proprio* by which the Discipline of First Tonsure, Minor Orders, and Subdiaconate in the Latin Church Is Reformed," Pope Paul VI, August 15, 1972, 6–11. "Apostolic Letter Issued *Motu Proprio* Laying Down Certain Norms Regarding the Holy Order of Deacons," Pope Paul VI, August 15, 1972, 31–38.

3. *Ibid.* "Apostolic Constitution: Approval of New Rites for the Ordination of Deacons, Presbyters and Bishops," Pope Paul VI, June 18, 1968, 44–48.

4. *Ibid.* 47.

5. Fr. A. M. Roguet, O.P., a liturgical writer in France who popularized the worship reforms wrote in 1953, "This is in keeping with the action of Christ who instituted both the Eucharist and Holy Orders simultaneously when he said 'Do this in commemoration of me,' at the last supper." *Christ Acts Through Sacraments*, p. 113. The revised ritual books and Church calendar implies acceptance of this concept by suggesting as a topic for the homily on Holy Thursday night one mystery commemorated in every celebration, "the institution of the priesthood." The Chrism Mass with its "Renewal of Commitment to Priestly Service," often celebrated on Holy Thursday, likewise seems to suggest this understanding.

6. Richard P. McBrien, *Catholicism* (Minneapolis: Winston Press, 1981) 802.

7. Joseph Martos, *Doors to the Sacred* 453–56. Nathan Mitchell, *Mission and Ministry* (Wilmington: Michael Glazier, Inc., 1982) 116–21.

8. McBrien, *Catholicism* 802.

9. Martos, *Doors to the Sacred* 455.

10. Mitchell, *Mission and Ministry* 198.

11. *Ibid.* 201.

12. *Ibid.* 258.

13. *Ibid.* 253.

14. Bishops' Committee on the Liturgy, *The Deacon: Minister of Word and Sacrament*. Study Text VI (Washington: Publications Office, United States Catholic Conference, 1979) 5.

15. Flannery, *Vatican Council II: The Conciliar and Post Conciliar Documents*, vol. 1 "Dogmatic Constitution on the Church," article 33, 390.

16. *The Rites* vol. II, article 7, 10.

17. *Code of Canon Law*, 1031.

18. August Franzen and John P. Dolan, *A History of the Church* (New York: Herder and Herder, 1968) 72.

19. Charles Poulet, *A History of the Catholic Church* (St. Louis: B. Herder Book Co., 1949) I, 142.

20. *Ibid.* 143.

21. John J. Dietzen, *The New Question Box* (Peoria: Guildhall Publishers, Ltd., 1981) 274.

22. Pope John Paul II, "A Letter to Priests." April 9, 1979 (See *Origins*, N C Documentary Service, Washington, vol. 8, no. 44, April 19, 1979, 696–704). Note also the statement on Ministerial Priesthood by the 1971 Synod of Bishops.

23. Susan M. DeMosi, "Commentary," *The Priest* (September 1985) 2.

24. Agnes Cunningham, *The Role of Women in Ecclesial Ministry: Biblical and Patristic Foundations* (Washington: Publications Office, United States Catholic Conference, 1976) 5.

25. *Ibid.* 7.

Chapter 9   Sacramentals: Connecting the Creator and Creation

1. Lawrence F. X. Brett, *Redeemed Creation: Sacramentals Today* (Wilmington: Michael Glazier, Inc., 1984) 13.

2. Richard P. McBrien, *Catholicism* (Minneapolis: Winston Press, 1981) 745.

3. *Code of Canon Law* 1166.

4. Austin Flannery, *Vatican Council II: The Conciliar and Post Conciliar Documents,* vol. 1 (Collegeville: The Liturgical Press, 1975) "The Constitution on the Sacred Liturgy," articles 60–61, p. 20.

5. McBrien, *Catholicism* 744–45.

6. *Code of Canon Law* 1167–1168.

7. Philip T. Weller, *The Roman Ritual* (Milwaukee: The Bruce Publishing Company, 1964) 764.

8. Flannery, *Vatican Council II: The Conciliar and Post Conciliar Documents,* vol. 1, "The Constitution on the Sacred Liturgy," article 62, p. 20.

9. *Ibid.* article 79, p. 23.

10. Brett, *Redeemed Creation: Sacramentals Today* 44–49.

11. Thomas G. Simons, *Blessings* (Saratoga, Calif.: Resource Publications, Inc., 1981).

12. Thomas G. Simons, *Blessings for God's People* (Notre Dame, Ind.: Ave Maria Press, 1983) 78–79.

13. *Code of Canon Law* 1168.

14. Brett, *Redeemed Creation: Sacramentals Today* 157–58.

15. Flannery, *Vatican Council II: The Conciliar and Post Conciliar Documents,* vol. 1, "Pastoral Constitution on the Church in the Modern World," article 1, p. 903.

Chapter 10   Seven Special Signs of Grace

1. Joseph Martos, *Doors to the Sacred* (Garden City, N.Y.: Doubleday and Company, 1981) 12–13.

2. *Ibid.* 22–26.

3. *Ibid.* 26.

4. *Webster's Third New International Dictionary* (Springfield, Mass.; G. and C. Merriam Company, 1976) 1996.

5. Martos, *Doors to the Sacred* 11.

6. *Ibid.* 11–12.

7. Richard P. McBrien, *Catholicism* (Minneapolis: Winston Press, 1981) 734.

8. Martos, *Doors to the Sacred* 36–42.

9. *Ibid.* 66–67.

10. *Ibid.* 68–69.

11. McBrien, *Catholicism* 745.

12. Ludwig Ott, *Fundamentals of Catholic Dogma* (St. Louis: B. Herder Book Company, 1954) 336.

13. Austin Flannery, *Vatican Council II: The Conciliar and Post Conciliar Documents*, vol. 1 "Constitution on the Sacred Liturgy," article 59, p. 20.

14. *Ibid.* article 21, p. 9.

15. *Ibid.* article 62, p. 20.

16. Joseph Martos, *The Catholic Sacraments* (Wilmington: Michael Glazier, Inc., 1983) 32.

17. McBrien, *Catholicism* 743–44.

18. William J. Bausch. *A New Look at the Sacraments* (West Mystic, Conn.: Twenty-Third Publications, 1977) 3–5.

19. Martos, *Doors to the Sacred* 31.

20. *Webster's Third New International Dictionary* 984.

21. Martos, *The Catholic Sacraments* 119–22.

22. Flannery, *Vatican Council II: The Conciliar and Post Conciliar Documents*, vol. 1, "Constitution on the Sacred Liturgy," article 59, p. 20.

23. Bishop's Committee on the Liturgy, National Conference of Catholic Bishops, *Music in Catholic Worship* (Washington: United States Catholic Conferences Publications Office, 1983, Revised Edition) 9–13.

24. Martos, *Doors to the Sacred* 140–43.

25. Flannery, *Vatican Council II: The Conciliar and Post Conciliar Documents*, vol. 1, "Constitution on the Sacred Liturgy," article 7, pp. 4–5.

26. Martos, *Doors to the Sacred* 143–46.

27. Martos, *The Catholic Sacraments* 133.

28. Flannery, *Vatican Council II: The Conciliar and Post Conciliar Documents*, vol. 1, "Constitution on the Sacred Liturgy," article 7, p. 5.

29. *Ibid.* article 26, p. 10.

30. *Ibid.* article 27, p. 11.

31. Martos, *The Catholic Sacraments* 134–35; *Doors to the Sacred* 148–50.

32. Martos, *Doors to the Sacred* 150.

33. Martos, *The Catholic Sacraments* 135–46.

34. *Ibid.* 139.

35. *Ibid.* 146–54.

36. *Ibid.* 152.

37. *Ibid.* 155–63.

38. *Ibid.* 162.

39. *Ibid.* 162.